The Four Generations of Entity Resolution

Synthesis Lectures on Data Management

Editor
H.V. Jagadish, *University of Michigan*

Founding Editor
M. Tamer Özsu, *University of Waterloo*

Synthesis Lectures on Data Management is edited by H.V. Jagadish of the University of Michigan. The series publishes 80–150 page publications on topics pertaining to data management. Topics include query languages, database system architectures, transaction management, data warehousing, XML and databases, data stream systems, wide scale data distribution, multimedia data management, data mining, and related subjects.

The Four Generations of Entity Resolution
George Papadakis, Ekaterini Ioannou, Emanouil Thanos, and Themis Palpanas
2021

Fault-Tolerant Distributed Transactions on Blockchain
Suyash Gupta, Jelle Hellings, and Mohammad Sadoghi
2021

Skylines and Other Dominance-Based Queries
Apostolos N. Papadopoulos, Eleftherios Tiakas, Theodoros Tzouramanis, Nikolaoes Georgiadis, and Yannis Manalopoulos
2020

Cloud-Based RDF Data Management
Zoi Kaoudi, Ioana Manolescu, and Stamatis Zampetakis
2020

Community Search over Big Graphs
Xin Huang, Laks V.S. Lakshmanan, and Jianliang Xu
2019

On Transactional Concurrency Control
Goetz Graefe
2019

The Four Generations of Entity Resolution

George Papadakis, Ekaterini Ioannou, Emanouil Thanos, and Themis Palpanas

ISBN: 978-3-031-00750-7   paperback
ISBN: 978-3-031-01878-7   ebook
ISBN: 978-3-031-00105-5   hardcover

DOI 10.1007/978-3-031-01878-7

A Publication in the Springer series
SYNTHESIS LECTURES ON DATA MANAGEMENT

Lecture #65
Series Editor: H.V. Jagadish, *University of Michigan*
Founding Editor: M. Tamer Özsu, *University of Waterloo*
Series ISSN
Print 2153-5418   Electronic 2153-5426

The Four Generations
of Entity Resolution

George Papadakis
National and Kapodistrian University of Athens, Greece

Ekaterini Ioannou
Tilburg University, Netherlands

Emanouil Thanos
Katholieke Universiteit Leuven, Belgium

Themis Palpanas
University of Paris, France & French University Institute (IUF), France

SYNTHESIS LECTURES ON DATA MANAGEMENT #65

ABSTRACT

Entity Resolution (ER) lies at the core of data integration and cleaning and, thus, a bulk of the research examines ways for improving its effectiveness and time efficiency. The initial ER methods primarily target Veracity in the context of structured (relational) data that are described by a schema of well-known quality and meaning. To achieve high effectiveness, they leverage schema, expert, and/or external knowledge. Part of these methods are extended to address Volume, processing large datasets through multi-core or massive parallelization approaches, such as the MapReduce paradigm. However, these early schema-based approaches are inapplicable to Web Data, which abound in voluminous, noisy, semi-structured, and highly heterogeneous information. To address the additional challenge of Variety, recent works on ER adopt a novel, loosely schema-aware functionality that emphasizes scalability and robustness to noise. Another line of present research focuses on the additional challenge of Velocity, aiming to process data collections of a continuously increasing volume. The latest works, though, take advantage of the significant breakthroughs in Deep Learning and Crowdsourcing, incorporating external knowledge to enhance the existing words to a significant extent.

This synthesis lecture organizes ER methods into four generations based on the challenges posed by these four Vs. For each generation, we outline the corresponding ER workflow, discuss the state-of-the-art methods per workflow step, and present current research directions. The discussion of these methods takes into account a historical perspective, explaining the evolution of the methods over time along with their similarities and differences. The lecture also discusses the available ER tools and benchmark datasets that allow expert as well as novice users to make use of the available solutions.

KEYWORDS

entity resolution, entity matching, blocking, clustering, data integration, data cleaning, data evolution

Contents

Preface

Entity Resolution (ER) lies at the core of data integration, cleaning, and querying. As a result, a bulk of the research examines ways for improving its effectiveness and time efficiency. Initially, the relevant methods were primarily crafted for addressing *Veracity* in the context of structured (relational) data that are described by a schema of well-known quality and meaning. To achieve high effectiveness, they typically relied on expert and/or external knowledge. Some of these methods were later extended to address *Volume*, processing large datasets through multi-core or massive parallelization approaches, such as the MapReduce paradigm. In the context of Web data, though, these schema-based approaches were inapplicable, as the scope of ER gradually moved toward voluminous, noisy, semi-structured, and highly heterogeneous data collections. To address the additional challenge of *Variety*, recent works on ER adopt a novel, loosely schema-aware functionality that emphasizes scalability and robustness to noise. Another line of recent approaches focuses on the additional challenge of *Velocity*, aiming to process data collections of continuously increasing volume through the ingestion of new information. The latest works take advantage of the significant breakthroughs in Deep Learning and Crowdsourcing, incorporating external knowledge to further enhance the performance of earlier approaches.

This synthesis lecture provides a generation-centric overview of ER. For each generation, we outline the corresponding ER workflow, discuss the state-of-the-art methods per workflow step, and present current and open research directions. The focus is not only on traditional solutions but also on the latest developments in the areas of non-structured, crowdsourced, incremental, progressive, and deep-learned solutions. In the discussion of these methods, we take into account a historical perspective, explaining the evolution of the methods over time, and pinpointing their similarities and differences. This book also discusses the available ER tools and benchmark datasets that allow experienced, as well as lay, practitioners to apply and assess the available solutions. In this way, we provide readers with a deep understanding of the broad field of ER, highlighting the landmarks in this active research domain.

George Papadakis, Ekaterini Ioannou, Emanouil Thanos, and Themis Palpanas
February 2021

Acknowledgments

We would like to thank all our collaborators (students and colleagues alike) for everything they have taught us.

George Papadakis, Ekaterini Ioannou, Emanouil Thanos, and Themis Palpanas
February 2021

CHAPTER 1

Entity Resolution: Past, Present, and Yet-to-Come

The core organizational unit in many applications is the *profile*, i.e., the collection of information that pertains to a particular real-world entity. Profiles are used to organize data of any structuredness, be it structured (e.g., relational databases), semi-structured (e.g., knowledge bases), or even unstructured (e.g., free text). For instance, the database of a bank uses profiles that describe clients, the knowledge graph of an on-line social network uses profiles about persons, locations, and events, and a recommendation application uses profiles about products described in plain text.

The semantics of profiles and the connections between them play a crucial role in the performance of a wide variety of applications that range from data analytics to query answering, object-oriented searching, and data evolution. Invariably, though, profiles are dirty, containing noisy, incorrect, redundant, or simply incomplete information. It is of paramount importance to integrate different profiles that actually describe the same real-world entity. For example, two banks that merge need to combine their customer databases so as to detect their shared clients along with the unique ones. This essential task is called *Entity Resolution* (**ER**).

Putting ER into practice entails a number of challenges that arise from the application settings, i.e., the data and system characteristics as well as the resource and time restrictions. The evolving nature of the settings implies a corresponding evolution of the challenges. This explains the plethora of methodologies that have been proposed to successfully apply ER in various domains. For this book, we studied how ER challenges evolved over the years and organized the work in this area into four generations of ER methods. Each generation focuses on addressing particular challenges, which we describe below. Figure 1.1 illustrates these four generations of ER methods on the horizontal axis along with the respective main challenges and their level of difficulty on the vertical axis.

The 1st generation comprises the initial ER methods that deal with textual differences in database records [Christen, 2012a]. These records involve various forms of inconsistencies, noise, or sparsity in profiles, which are introduced during the manual data entry, or by the limitations of the automatic extraction techniques. They are described by schemata of known semantics and quality, their size is moderate, and they are mostly static, i.e., their evolution is typically considered slow and, thus, irrelevant. In this context, the main challenge for ER is *Veracity*, i.e., achieving high accuracy despite the high profile noise. Veracity is addressed by leveraging

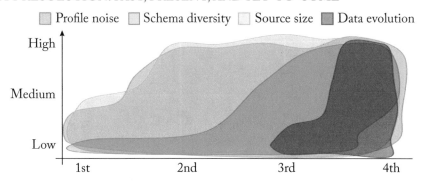

Figure 1.1: Illustration of the challenges along with their corresponding level that are addressed by the four generations of ER.

schema and domain knowledge and/or labeled instances to automatically learn matching rules that simultaneously maximize precision and recall. A workflow consisting of two core steps is typically used: first, the obviously unrelated profiles are quickly discarded, and then the related profiles are detected based on the *similarity assumption*, i.e., the more similar two profiles are, the more likely they are to refer to the same entity, and vice versa.

The 2nd generation focuses on the combined effect of Veracity and *Volume*, as the size of the input now raises up to several million profiles. Given that the rest of the challenges remain similar, there is no significant change in the logic of ER methods. Emphasis is placed, though, on increasing its throughput. This is achieved through parallelization, from multicore to GPU parallel processing. Most efforts, though, focus on the recent paradigm for *massive paralleliza-tion*, namely Map/Reduce. In this context, special care is taken to avoid the underutilization of computational resources through Load Balancing techniques.

In the 3rd generation, Veracity and Volume persist and are accompanied by extreme schema diversity, a challenge called *Variety*. The scope of ER has moved to semi-structured or even unstructured Web data, which is dominated by user-generated content. Instead of a database-like schema, there is an unprecedented level of schema noise and heterogeneity as well as loose schema bindings of unclear semantics. For example, there are ∼2,600 different vocabularies in the Link Open Data cloud,[1] but only 109 from them are shared by more than one dataset [Efthymiou et al., 2019]. Inevitably, the schema-aware methods of the previous generations are inapplicable in these settings. Instead, schema-agnostic methods have been amalgamated into a comprehensive end-to-end workflow. This waives the need for expert and domain knowledge, yet it is quite effective and time efficient, especially when leveraging the various parallelization schemes for higher scalability.

---

[1]https://lod-cloud.net

More recently, the 4th generation tackles the additional challenge of Velocity, which emanates from the continuously increasing volume of input data. To address this challenge, novel progressive methods and workflows produce useful results in a pay-as-you-go manner, before the full completion of ER. Velocity also stems from constraints related to response time, which needs to be low. Query-driven ER resolves profiles while answering to an incoming query profile, whereas Incremental ER refines existing results as new, possibly conflicting evidence becomes available by focusing on a portion of the overall datasets—rather than repeating the entire ER process from scratch.

Even though these generations are more or less numbered by order of appearance, none of them has become obsolete so far. Generation 4 is not the sole focus of research. Instead, all generations are actively being investigated at the moment, especially in relation to the recent, promising developments in Deep Learning and Crowdsourcing. Deep Learning (DL) incorporates complex classification models and powerful pre-trained representations of textual evidence in profiles, while crowdsourcing devises efficient and effective techniques for leveraging human feedback. These two forms of external knowledge can be applied to any workflow step in any generation, improving their performance to a significant extent. These directions are actively being investigated at the moment.

Existing Surveys and Our Contributions. Several surveys and books have already examined various aspects of ER. They focus, though, on a particular generation and/or a particular workflow step. For example, for Generation 1, the main Blocking methods are surveyed in Christen [2012b], the main Matching methods in Getoor and Machanavajjhala [2012], Köpcke and Rahm [2010], Köpcke et al. [2010], and Koudas et al. [2006], while the entire ER workflow for this generation is covered in Christen [2012a] and Elmagarmid et al. [2007], Blocking across all generations is outlined in Papadakis et al. [2020b], whereas Christophides et al. [2015, 2020] and Naumann and Herschel [2010] discuss mostly methods from Generation 3, and Dong and Srivastava [2015] looks into the main methods for Generations 2 and 3.

This work has several differences to the existing ones. First, it groups ER methods into generations, a novel categorization that is based on the typically used aspects of Big Data [Dong and Srivastava, 2015]. This allows for faster navigation to the ER method(s) that can be used for a particular situation or setting. Second, this book is the first one to examine the recent developments in DL and crowdsourcing for ER in a systematic and thorough way. Special care is also taken to present the open-source ER tools along with the established benchmark datasets, facilitating researchers and practitioners to put the main ER approaches into practice.

Outline of the book. The remaining manuscript is organized as follows. Chapter 2 defines the particular task, while Chapters 3–6 elaborate on the four generations, analyzing the respective ER workflow along with the main approaches per workflow step. Chapter 7 discusses the recent advances in deep learning and crowdsourced ER, and Chapter 8 gives an overview of related resources. We conclude in Chapter 9 with a list of possible directions for future work.

CHAPTER 2

Preliminaries

This chapter formally defines the ER task and its core notions along with the measures used for evaluating the generated results. The following definitions and notations are generic and can capture the variations of this problem across the different domains (e.g., in structured and semi-structured data).

The fundamental component of the ER data model is the *profile*, also known as *instance*, *entity description*, or *reference*. Each profile provides information about a particular real-world object, such as an event, location, organization, or person. More formally:

Definition 2.1   A **profile** p_i is a subset of a data source DS, i.e., $p_i \subset DS$, providing information about a real-world object. An **entity** e_k is a set of profiles, i.e., $e_k = \{p_1, \ldots, p_n\}$, where all $p_i, \ldots, p_n$ pertain to the same real-world object. ∎

Existing methods use different profile definitions, depending on the data format in the given data source. For example, in the case of a relational database, we could have $p_i = R$ $(a_1, \ldots, a_k)$, where R denotes the name of the relation and $a_1, \ldots, a_k$ its attributes. In the case of semi-structured data, we could have profiles corresponding to a set of attribute-value pairs $p_i = \{(a_l, v_m)\}$. The latter definition is more flexible with respect to the schema describing a profile, as it supports a heterogeneous set of attribute names, multiple values for the same attribute, as well as tag-style values, which lack an attribute.

Any pair of profiles from an entity e_k, i.e., (p_i, p_j) s.t. $p_i, p_j \in e_k$, is commutative, transitive, symmetric, and reflexive. To ease notation, in the remaining text, such a pair is denoted with $\mathbf{p_i} \equiv \mathbf{p_j}$, and we refer to it using interchangeably the terms **match** and **duplicate**.

The data sources are typically classified according to the number of profiles in each entity. A data source containing at most one profile per entity is called *Clean DS*, whereas one containing multiple profiles per entity is called *Dirty DS*. More formally:

Definition 2.2   A data source is a **Dirty DS** if $\exists\, e_k = \{p_i, \ldots, p_j\}$ s.t. $p_i, \ldots, p_j \in DS$, or a **Clean DS** if $\nexists\, e_k = \{p_i, \ldots, p_j\}$ s.t. $p_i, \ldots, p_j \in DS$. ∎

In this context, ER is formally defined as follows [Christophides et al., 2015]:

Problem Statement 2.3   The **Entity Resolution** task aims to generate entities from the profiles included in a set of data sources S. The task is called **Dirty ER** if S includes a single Dirty DS, **Clean-Clean ER** if S encompasses exactly two Clean DSs, and **Multi-source ER** if S comprises multiple DSs, i.e., $|S| \geq 2$.

Example 2.4   Figure 2.1 illustrates a Clean-Clean ER task over structured data. Figure 2.1a depicts the data source D, which conveys author data that is described by three textual attributes of high quality; Figure 2.1b shows the data source W, which involves census data that is described by four textual attributes and a numeric one ("Age")—three of them with missing values; and Figure 2.1c shows the ER result, with every entity including at most one profile from each data source.

A Dirty ER task over structured data is illustrated in Figure 2.2. The original set of profiles in the input data source G is shown in Figure 2.2a. Each profile involves five attributes, three textual, and two numeric ones. The final set of entities appears in Figure 2.2b. Unlike Clean-Clean ER, the size of every entity e_k is arbitrary, $|e_k| \geq 1$.

Finally, a multi-source ER task over structured data is illustrated in Figure 2.3. It includes three different data sources combining data from the two previous cases, as shown in Figure 2.3a. The final set of entities appears in Figure 2.3b.

Typically, ER methods depend on the characteristics of input data. In case a given DS is described by a well-defined schema (e.g., a relational database), its profiles convey schema information that can be used during resolution. Techniques exploiting such information are known as **schema-aware** or **schema-based** ER methods. The opposite situation involves data sources lacking a schema or described by a noisy and heterogeneous schema. Such a schema may be ignored by ER techniques, which are thus called **schema-agnostic** or **schema-independent**.

In some environments, expert knowledge or mere heuristics are available. Such information can become useful by being incorporated into **non-learning** ER methods. In contrast, **learning-based** ER methods use machine learning techniques to train models for solving the problem. These techniques are further distinguished into **unsupervised** methods, which require no labeled data, and **supervised** ones, which employ labeled data in the form of matching and non-matching profiles, called *positive* and *negative instances*, respectively. Arguably, the biggest limitation of supervised approaches is the requirement for an *a priori* labeled dataset in order to train the selected learning algorithm to classify new instances, similar to the ones met in the training set.

Regardless of the input DSs and their characteristics, ER relies on matching functions, which estimate the *similarity* between two profiles, p_i and p_j. The similarity, which is also referred to as *resemblance* and *matching probability*, is used to decide whether two profiles should be included in the same entity, i.e., if $p_i \equiv p_j$ and $p_i \in e_k$ then $e_k = e_k \cup \{p_j\}$. More formally:

Definition 2.5   Given two profiles p_i and p_j, their *similarity* is determined by a **Matching Function**, denoted as $c_{i,j}|p_i, p_j \mapsto [0, 1]$. An **Oracle** is a matching function that decides with 100% accuracy whether p_i and p_j are matching or not.   ∎

Having an Oracle is of course ideal, but usually unrealistic. In practice, the majority of ER methods approximate the Oracle by using one or more similarity measures along with a threshold

id	Name	Surname	Organization
D1	Robert	Smith	University of California
D2	Joan	Clarke	University of Buenos Aires
D3	Anthony H.	Kane	City, University of London
D4	Joe	Green	PSL University, Paris
D5	Serge	Lenglet	New York University
D6	Jack	Smyth	New York University
D7	Ann	Green	University of Athens
D8	David	York	University of Münster
D9	Luc	Vander Bollen	ULB, Brussels
D10	Argyrios	Samaris	UPV, Valencia

(a)

id	Name	Surname	Age	City	Country
W1	Antony	Kane		London	UK
W2	Dave	York	33		
W3	Bob	Smith			USA
W4	Jack	Smith	56	New York City	USA
W5	Joanne	Clark	68		
W6	Joe	Green	59	Paris	France
W7	Annabelles	Greenwood	49		Canada
W8	Luke	van der Bollen		Brussels	Belgium

(b)

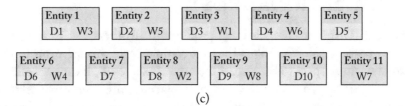

(c)

Figure 2.1: An example of Clean-Clean ER over *structured* data: (a)–(b) the input DSs and (c) the corresponding entities.

id	Name	Affiliation	Areas of Interest	#Articles	#Citations
G1	Robert Smith	University of California	Artificial Intelligence, Text Mining	25	1602
G2	Joan Clarke	University of Buenos Aires	Entomology	12	441
G3	Anthony H. Kane	City, University of London	Database	9	41
G4	Joe Green	PSL University, Paris	Computer Science, Algorithms	149	6221
G5	Joanne Clark	University of Buenos Aires	Entomology	12	429
G6	Annabelles Greenwood	University of Toronto	Algorithms	2	1
G7	Robert Smith	University of California	Database, Text Mining	26	1610
G8	Antony Kane	Unknown	Biological Databases	9	39
G9	Serge Lenglet	New York University	Entomology	22	2291
G10	Antony Kane	City, University of London	Bioinformatics	5	26

(a)

Entity 1	Entity 2	Entity 3	Entity 4	Entity 5	Entity 6
G1 G7	G2 G5	G3 G8 G10	G4	G6	G9

(b)

Figure 2.2: An example of Dirty ER over *structured* data: (a) the input DS and (b) the corresponding entities.

θ such that $c_{i,j} \geq \theta \Rightarrow p_i \equiv p_j$. A $c_{i,j}$ with a result that does not distinguish between a match or non-match is called **uncertain match**. In these cases, the ER method typically leverages additional information to reach a decision.

2.1 COMPUTATIONAL COST

In the worst case, ER needs to compare every profile with all others, i.e., to apply the Matching function to every possible pair of profiles. The time complexity of this naive, brute-force solution to ER is quadratic with respect to the size of the input. As a result, it cannot scale to large data sources [Christen, 2012a]. To reduce the computational cost of ER to manageable and scalable levels, **Blocking** is typically used. Its goal is to group together similar profiles into clusters, called *blocks*, such that comparisons are executed only inside each block. In this way, the time complexity is now quadratic to the size of the blocks, which is much smaller than the size of the input DSs.

The relative cost of these approaches is illustrated in Figure 2.4, which pertains to a Dirty ER task with N profiles as input. The brute-force approach corresponds to the grey area ($N \cdot (N-1)/2$), while the red circle indicates the minimum possible computational cost, in the ideal

Profile	Name	Surname	Organization
D1	Robert	Smith	University of California
D2	Joan	Clarke	University of Buenos Aires
D3	Anthony H.	Kane	City, University of London
D4	Joe	Green	PSL University, Paris
D5	Serge	Lenglet	New York University

Profile	Name	Surname	Age	City	Country
W1	Antony	Kane		London	UK
W2	Dave	Johnson	33		
W3	Bob	Smith			USA
W4	Jack	Smith	56	New York City	USA

Profile	Name	Affiliation	#Articles	#Citations
G1	Robert Smith	University of California	25	1602
G2	Joan Clarke	University of Buenos Aires	12	441
G3	Anthony H. Kane	City, University of London	9	41
G4	Joe Green	PSL University, Paris	149	6221

(a)

Entity 1		
D1	W3	G1

Entity 2	
D2	G2

Entity 3		
D3	W1	G3

Entity 4	
D4	G4

Entity 5
D5

Entity 6
W2

Entity 7
W4

(b)

Figure 2.3: An example of Multi-source ER over *structured* data: (a) the input DSs and (b) the corresponding entities.

case that we exclusively compare the matching profiles. The green circle represents the cost of Blocking, which covers the largest part of duplicate pairs, but not all of them, as it typically constitutes an *approximate procedure* based on heuristics (i.e., it cannot guarantee to detect all duplicates). The closer the two circles are, the more effective is Blocking.

Blocking represents each profile by one or more signatures, which are called *blocking keys*. Then, it places into blocks all profiles having the same or similar blocking keys. More formally:

Definition 2.6 Given a set of sources, i.e., $DS_1, \ldots, DS_k$, a **blocking scheme** B^{key} generates a set of blocks $\{b_1^{key}, \ldots, b_n^{key}\}$ through the **blocking key** key. Each **block** b_i^{key} is a subset of the profiles from the given data sources that have the same (or similar) value for key, i.e., $b_i^{key} \subset \bigcup_{j=1}^{k} DS_j$. ∎

Example 2.7 Figure 2.5 illustrates a simple blocking scheme applied to the Clean-Clean DSs of Figure 2.1. The values of attribute "Surname" are used as blocking keys to form the resulting

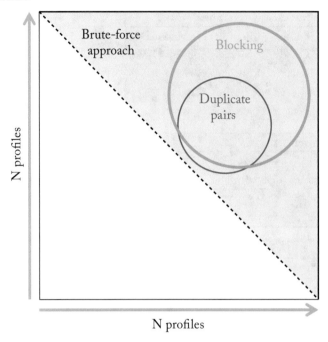

Figure 2.4: The relative computational cost for the brute-force approach, Blocking and the ideal solution (Duplicate Pairs) in the case of Dirty ER, based on Papadakis et al. [2020b].

Smith			Green			Kane			York		
D1	W3		D4	W6		D3	W1		D8	W2	
	W4		D7				W4				

Figure 2.5: A simple blocking scheme applied to the Clean DSs of Figure 2.1.

blocks. The resulting blocks involve just $(2 + 1 + 1 + 1 =)$ 5 comparisons, a computational cost that is significantly lower than the $(10 \times 8 =)$ 80 comparisons of the brute-force approach.

Existing ER methods apply different Blocking mechanisms based on the challenges of the given data. As we will discuss in following sections, we have ER methods with mechanisms for generating non-overlapping blocks (i.e., $\forall b_i^{key}, b_j^{key} \in B^{key} : b_i^{key} \cap b_j^{key} \neq \emptyset$), selecting the most beneficial order for processing blocks, deciding when to stop processing blocks, etc.

2.2   PERFORMANCE EVALUATION

To assess the **effectiveness** of ER methods, the following measures are typically considered.

- *True Positive (TP)* gives the number of matched profiles that indeed correspond to the same entity.

- *False Positive (FP)* gives the number of matched profiles that actually correspond to different entities.

- *False Negative (FN)* gives the number of non-matched profiles that actually correspond to the same entity.

On this basis, the following three measures are defined in the interval $[0, 1]$, with higher values indicating higher effectiveness.

1. *Precision* measures the portion of correctly matched profiles: $Pr = \dfrac{TP}{TP + FP}$.

2. *Recall* measures the portion of detected matches: $Re = \dfrac{TP}{TP + FN}$.

3. *F-Measure* is the harmonic mean of Precision and Recall: $F1 = \dfrac{2 \cdot Pr \cdot Re}{Pr + Re}$.

F-Measure is typically used as the single measure summarizing all aspects of the effectiveness of an ER approach. This practice, though, has been challenged in Hand and Christen [2018], which argues that the F-Measure is also equivalent to an arithmetic mean of recall and precision, with the actual weights between the two depending on the method at hand. An alternative measure, called *Generalized Merge Distance*, has been proposed in Menestrina et al. [2010]. Inspired from the edit distance of strings, it essentially measures the merge and split operations that are required to transform the detected into the perfect results.

Note also that evaluating the actual effectiveness of an ER pipeline or system with respect to the above measures might be challenging. Due to the heavy imbalance between matching and non-matching pairs of profiles (in favor of the latter), a statistically sound approach is required for sampling the ER output. This is offered by *OASIS* [Marchant and Rubinstein, 2017], an open-source system that implements a principled and efficient approach based on a stratified Bayesian generative model.

The **time efficiency** of ER methods is typically measured through their *overall run-time*, i.e., the time that intervenes between receiving the input profiles and returning the detected entities as output. In practice, this run-time depends largely on the effectiveness of the blocking method that is employed.

To assess the quality of a blocking scheme B^{key} independently of the performance of the subsequent steps like Matching, it is generally assumed that a pair of duplicates is detected as long as they co-occur in at least one block [Christen, 2012b, Dong and Srivastava, 2015, Papadakis et al., 2013, 2014a, Stefanidis et al., 2017]. Given a block b_i, the set of **candidate matches** (i.e., pairs of profiles to be compared) is denoted by $MC(b_i) = \{c_{k,l} : p_k \in b_i \wedge p_l \in b_i\}$, while the set of true entities, to which the given profiles belong, is denoted by $E(b_i) =$

$\{p_i \equiv p_j : p_k \in b_i \wedge p_l \in b_i\}$ [Christen, 2012b, Dong and Srivastava, 2015, Stefanidis et al., 2017].

The size of $E(b_i)$ relates to effectiveness, since it bounds the number of entities that are correctly detected by the overall ER process. The size of $MC(b_i)$ relates to time efficiency, as it determines the number of executed matching functions. Intuitively, a larger $MC(b_i)$ yields a larger $E(b_i)$, though at a higher computational cost, due to the additional comparisons that should be executed. Given that a mere subset of the executed matching functions in MC correspond to valid entities in E, a blocking scheme is considered successful as long as it achieves a good balance between the two sets. This trade-off is commonly captured by the following three measures, which are all defined in the interval $[0, 1]$, with higher values indicating higher effectiveness [Bilenko et al., 2006, de Vries et al., 2009, Michelson and Knoblock, 2006, Papadakis et al., 2011b].

1. *Pair Completeness*, adapted from recall, denotes the portion of existing entities that are detected in the blocks of blocking scheme B^{key}:
   $PC(B^{key}) = \frac{|E \cap MC|}{|E|}$, where $E = \bigcup_{b_i \in B^{key}} E(b_i)$, $MC = \bigcup_{b_i \in B^{key}} MC(b_i)$.

2. *Pairs Quality*, adapted from precision, denotes the portion of candidate matches in the blocks of B^{key} that correspond to valid entities:
   $PQ(B^{key}) = \frac{|E \cap MC|}{|MC|}$.

3. *Reduction Ratio* expresses the reduction in the number of executed comparisons in the blocks of B^{key} with respect to the brute-force approach:
   $RR(B^{key}) = 1 - \frac{|MC|}{|BF|}$, where $|BF| = |DS_1| \times |DS_2|$ in case of Clean-Clean ER over the data sources DS_1 and DS_2, or $|BF| = \frac{|DS| \times (|DS|-1)}{2}$ in case of Dirty ER over the data source DS.

Example 2.8   In the example blocks of Figure 2.5, the set of candidate matches comprises the following pairs: $MC = \{(D_1, W_3), (D_1, W_4), (D_7, W_6), (D_8, W_2), (D_3, W_1)\}$. The corresponding set of entities, which appears in Figure 2.1c, comprises the following profile pairs: $E = \{(D_1, W_3), (D_2, W_5), (D_3, W_1), (D_4, W_6), (D_6, W_4), (D_8, W_2), (D_9, W_8)\}$. Note that E by definition, excludes the *singleton entities* that consist of a single profile—every entity that is not compared to any other is considered as a singleton entity. The set of common pairs is $E \cap MC = \{(D_1, W_3), (D_8, W_2)\}$ and the performance measures of Blocking take the following values:

$PC(B) = |E \cap MC|/|E| = 2/7 = 0.2857$,
$PQ(B) = |E \cap MC|/|MC| = 2/5 = 0.40$,
$RR(B) = 1 - |MC|/(|DS_1| \times |DS_2|) = 1 - 5/(10 \times 8) = 1 - 1/16 = 0.9375$.

We observe that the selected blocking scheme performs a deep pruning of the search space (very high RR) at the cost of very low recall (PC) and moderate precision (PQ).

It should be stressed at this point that ER is typically preceded by *Data Cleaning*, a preprocessing step that improves the quality of the input DSs, by reducing their noise. ER is also succeeded by *Data Fusion*, i.e., the task of merging duplicate profiles into a clean entity by resolving the conflicting information and synthesizing the complementary one. Both tasks lie out of the scope of this book. For more details on Data Cleaning and Data Fusion, please refer to Ilyas and Chu [2019] and to Bleiholder and Naumann [2008] and Dong and Naumann [2009], respectively.

CHAPTER 3

Generation 1: Addressing Veracity

The target of the ER methods in this generation is *Veracity*. They focus on transforming the input profiles into an accurate set of entities that is as close as possible to the corresponding real-world objects. Their input typically comprises structured data that are *homogeneous* or involve low levels of schema diversity. In the latter case, the attributes can be homogenized through a manual or automatic process. Hence, this generation primarily targets noise in the attribute values of profiles, operating in a schema-aware fashion. Depending on the input, this task is usually called **Record Linkage** or **Deduplication** [Christen, 2012a,b]. These terms are synonyms with Clean-Clean and Dirty ER, respectively, and can be used interchangeably with them.

Methods of this generation have been in use since the infancy of ER [Fellegi and Sunter, 1969], but remain at the core of recent methods (e.g., Reyes-Galaviz et al. [2017]) and cutting edge tools [Konda et al., 2016]. We can organize them according to the end-to-end ER workflow in Figure 3.1, which consists of the following steps.

1. *Schema Alignment* is an optional step needed only for Record Linkage over disparate schemata. Its goal is to create alignments between the attributes of the given DSs based on their relatedness, which is inferred from the similarity of their structure, name, and/or included values [Bernstein et al., 2011, Madhavan et al., 2001]. Identifying semantically equivalent attributes (e.g., "profession"-"job") enables the schema-aware operation of the next steps.

2. *Blocking* is necessary for reducing the quadratic time complexity of the naive, brute-force ER approach that compares every profile with all others—a process that cannot scale to large data sources [Christen, 2012a]. It restricts the candidate matches to pairs of profiles that are similar according to some criterion (e.g., common zip code for personal addresses). As a result, it boosts the overall time efficiency at the cost of an approximate solution—the more comparisons it filters out, the more duplicates are likely to be missed.

3. *Matching* performs the comparisons determined by Blocking, applying a Matching Function to the candidate matches [Elmagarmid et al., 2007]. The resulting degrees of similarity along with contextual information (e.g., the match decision of related profiles) are used to assign profile pairs into one of three possible categories, i.e., `match`, `non-match`, and `uncertain` (cf. Section 2).

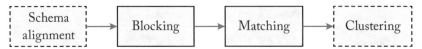

Figure 3.1: Illustration of the 1st generation end-to-end ER workflow. Dashed contours indicate optional steps.

4. *Clustering* is an optional step that goes beyond the local evidence encapsulated in the individual decisions or similarity scores. It leverages their global, collective information to infer indirect matching relations and to discard unlikely matches in favor of pairs with higher matching likelihood.

Next, we delve into the methods corresponding to each workflow component.

3.1   SCHEMA ALIGNMENT

The methods of this step leverage the attribute values in profiles as well as the available, if any, schema knowledge. The goal is to learn and use *attribute mappings* between the data sources, also called *transformations*, *correspondences*, or *rules* [Tejada et al., 2002, Yan et al., 2001]. To this end, *Active Atlas* [Tejada et al., 2002] starts with a collection of generic transformations (e.g., *abbreviation* for transforming "3rd" to "third," *acronym* for transforming "United Kingdom" to "UK") and learns the weight of each transformation given a particular application domain.

Example 3.1   Consider the following simple schema alignment rule: "*Two attributes are aligned if their names are identical.*" When applied to the Clean DSs of Figure 2.1, it identifies the attributes pairs: $< DS1.Name, DS2.Name >$ and
$< DS1.Surname, DS2.Surname >$ as semantically equivalent.

Another option is finding similarities between the profile values and relationships among these values [Melnik et al., 2002, Zhang et al., 2011]. For instance, the *similarity flooding* algorithm [Melnik et al., 2002] converts the given data into directed labeled graphs, where the nodes correspond to the schema elements and the edges to the relations between them. The algorithm then detects if the nodes in one graph are similar to the nodes in the second graph, while also propagating the found similarities to the respective neighbor nodes.

There are also methods going beyond schema and value processing. One such direction is the combination of different schema alignment methods, i.e., merging the results from previous alignment operations. This can be done using machine-based approaches, such as Doan et al. [2002], or generic approaches, such as Do and Rahm [2002] and Raffio et al. [2008].

Another direction is based on mapping composition. For example, the work in Madhavan and Halevy [2003] models the relationships between schemata. The work in Fuxman et al. [2006] creates mappings in a recursive manner: first, it defines how the top components of a schema relate, then it defines how their sub-components relate, and so forth. The resulting mappings are referred to as *nested mappings*.

Other methods are also based on machine learning mechanisms. Ehrig et al. [2005] introduces a machine learning approach that explores the user validation of initial alignments for optimizing alignment methods. *GLUE* [Doan et al., 2002] creates alignments in a semi-automatic way between the schemata, whereas *LSD* [Doan et al., 2001] creates alignments between the schema and a mediated schema. GLUE first applies a set of learners and then it combines the results they generate. User assistance is leveraged in Lee et al. [2007] in order to improve the quality of the outcomes generated by the automatic part of the solution.

Other methods focused on automated or semi-automated tools for creating schema mappings. One such example is the *Clio* system [Hernández et al., 2001], which operates without making assumptions about the relationship between the schemata or how they were created. The automatic tuning of the schema matching of the *eTuner* system [Lee et al., 2007] also belongs to this category. Finally, the *Valentine* suite[1] implements the main methods of this generation. It is used in Koutras et al. [2020] to perform and analyze a detailed comparative experimental study.

3.2   BLOCKING

This step receives as input the original DS(s) along with the output of Schema Alignment (if applicable) and clusters together similar profiles into blocks, which are returned as output. In this way, Matching suffices to compare only the candidate matches inside the blocks.

Internally, Blocking operates in a *schema-aware* fashion, assuming that the input data adheres to a known schema or to aligned schemata. Based on this assumption and respective domain knowledge, the most suitable attributes are used for extracting one or more representative signatures from each profile. These signatures are called *blocking keys* and are composed of (combinations of) parts of values from the most informative attributes. Assuming that these keys reflect the overall similarity of profile pairs, profiles with identical or similar keys are placed into the same block to be compared by Matching [Christen, 2012b].

Depending on how they define blocking keys, Blocking methods are distinguished into *local* and *global* ones. The former rely exclusively on the content of individual profiles, whereas the latter consider collective information from the entire input DS(s) or even from external sources. Each category involves several subcategories, as shown in the taxonomy of Figure 3.2.

3.2.1   LOCAL BLOCKING METHODS

Most methods of this type operate as hash functions: they associate every profile with one or more blocking keys and for every distinct key they create a separate block that contains all cor-

---

[1]https://delftdata.github.io/valentine

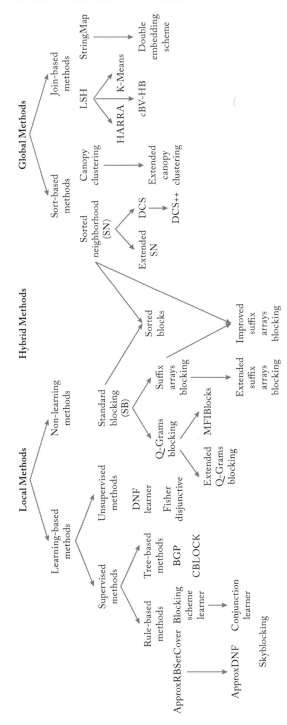

Figure 3.2: The taxonomy of 1st-generation Blocking methods, with the arrows pointing from the original method to its improvement.

responding profiles. We distinguish them into non-learning and learning-based methods, with the latter further categorized into supervised and unsupervised ones.

Non-learning Methods.   The cornerstone method here is *Standard Blocking* (SB) [Fellegi and Sunter, 1969], which requires an expert to manually define a part or a transformation of one or more attribute values as the single *blocking key* of each profile. Every profile is then placed in the block corresponding to its blocking key. This hash-based functionality results in *disjoint blocks*, thus being quite sensitive to noise in blocking keys—duplicates with the slightest difference in their keys share no block. To increase its robustness, a multi-pass functionality is applied in practice, i.e., SB is combined with several different definitions of blocking keys.

SB's sensitivity is also addressed by two families of local methods.

1. *Suffix Arrays Blocking* [Aizawa and Oyama, 2005] converts each SB key into the suffixes that are longer than a specific minimum length $l_{\min}$. Then, it defines a block for every suffix that does not exceed a predetermined frequency threshold $f_{\max}$, which specifies the maximum block size.

   Extended Suffix Arrays Blocking [Christen, 2012b, Papadakis et al., 2015] considers all substrings (not just the suffixes) with more than $l_{\min}$ characters so as to support noise at the end of SB keys (e.g., "JohnSnith" and "JohnSmith").

2. *Q-grams Blocking* [Christen, 2012b, Papadakis et al., 2015] converts SB keys into subsequences of q characters (*q-grams*) and defines a block for every distinct q-gram. *Extended Q-Grams Blocking* [Baxter et al., 2003, Christen, 2012b, Papadakis et al., 2015] concatenates multiple q-grams to form more distinctive blocking keys that yield higher precision (PQ) for similar recall (PC). *MFIBlocks* [Kenig and Gal, 2013] concatenates q-grams into itemsets and uses a maximal frequent itemset algorithm to detect those exceeding a predetermined support threshold. These itemsets are then used as the new blocking keys.

Example 3.2   An example applying two local, non-learning blocking methods to the Dirty DS in Figure 2.2 is shown in Figure 3.3. Standard Blocking defines as blocking key the concatenation of the following three pieces of information: (i) {"Name," Last2Characters}, (ii) {"Areas of Interest," First3Characters}, and (iii) {"#Citations," FirstCharacter}. The information extracted from each profile is highlighted in blue in Figure 3.3a. The resulting SB keys appear in Figure 3.3b, while the keys of Q-grams Blocking with $q = 4$ are shown in Figure 3.3c. Each key that is shared by more than two profiles produces a block. However, all Standard Blocking keys are unique, due to differences in the considered attribute values, thus yielding no block at all. In contrast, 4-Grams Blocking yields the blocks in Figure 3.3d, which involve three pair-wise comparisons and two duplicates. Hence, their precision is $PQ = 2/3 = 0.67$, while their recall is $PC = 2/5 = 0.4$.

id	Name	Affiliation	Areas of Interest	#Articles	#Citations
G1	Robert Smith	University of California	Artificial Intelligence, Text Mining	25	1602
G2	Joan Clarke	University of Buenos Aires	Entomology	12	441
G3	Anthony H. Kane	City, University of London	Database	9	41
G4	Joe Green	PSL University, Paris	Computer Science, Algorithms	149	6221
G5	Joanne Clark	University of Buenos Aires	Entomology	12	429
G6	Annabelles Greenwood	University of Toronto	Algorithms	2	1
G7	Robert Smith	University of California	Database, Text Mining	26	1610
G8	Antony Kane	Unknown	Biological Databases	9	39
G9	Serge Lenglet	New York University	Entomology	22	2291
G10	Antony Kane	City, University of London	Bioinformatics	5	26

(a)

id	Key
G1	thArt1
G2	keEnt4
G3	neDat4
G4	enCom6
G5	rkEnt4
G6	odAlg1
G7	thDat1
G8	neBio3
G9	etEnt2
G10	neBio2

(b)

id	Key
G1	thAr, hArt, Art1
G2	keEn, eEnt, **Ent4**
G3	neDa, eDat, Dat4
G4	enCo, nCom, Com6
G5	rkEn, kEnt, **Ent4**
G6	odAl, dAlg, Alg1
G7	thDa, hDat, Dat1
G8	**neBi, eBio,** Bio3
G9	etEn, tEnt, Ent2
G10	**neBi, eBio,** Bio2

(c)

Ent4
G2
G5

neBi
G8
G10

eBio
G8
G10

(d)

Figure 3.3: Applying Standard and 4-grams Blocking to the Dirty DS of Figure 2.2: (a) the input DS with highlighted the information used in blocking keys, (b) the blocking keys of Standard Blocking per profile, (c) the blocking keys of 4-grams Blocking per profile, and (d) the blocks of 4-grams Blocking—Standard Blocking yields no blocks.

Supervised Learning-based Methods. These methods yield *blocking schemes* composed of complex *predicates*, i.e., combinations of transformation functions that extract a blocking key from the value of a specific attribute, e.g., {title, First3Characters}. Since there are numerous alternative schemes, these methods try to learn the optimal one based on an objective function. They differ in two respects: (i) the form of the blocking schemes and/or (ii) the objective function.

Disjunctive blocking schemes are learned by *ApproxRBSetCover* [Bilenko et al., 2006], which solves a weighted set cover problem, where some positive instances may remain uncovered. Its objective function maximizes the ratio of the previously uncovered positive pairs over the covered negative pairs. The same objective function is optimized by *ApproxDNF* [Bilenko et al., 2006], which learns blocking schemes with up to k predicates in Disjunctive Normal Form (DNF). *Blocking Scheme Learner* [Michelson and Knoblock, 2006] learns a disjunction of conjunctions of predicates by minimizing the number of comparisons, while maintaining recall above a predetermined threshold. This is improved by *Conjunction Learner* [Cao et al., 2011], which minimizes the candidate matches not only in the labeled, but also in the *unlabeled* data (semi-supervised approach). *Skyblocking* [Shao et al., 2018] jointly learns multiple conjunctive and/or disjunctive blocking schemes under various performance constraints.

Other methods employ a tree representation of predicates. In *BGP* [Evangelista et al., 2010], the leaf nodes correspond to predicates, and a random set of blocking schemes is used for bootstrapping the learning process. These schemes are iteratively refined through a set of genetic programming operators that optimize a fitness function based on recall and the resulting number of comparisons. In *CBLOCK* [Sarma et al., 2012], every tree edge is annotated with a hash function, and every node n_i comprises the set of profiles that result after applying all hash functions from the root to n_i. Every node with more profiles than the maximum block size is split into smaller, disjoint blocks through a greedy algorithm, which picks the hash function that optimizes recall.

3.2.2   GLOBAL BLOCKING METHODS

Methods of this type rely on the similarity evidence that is extracted from the blocking keys of pairs of profiles, from the entire input DS(s), or even from the next workflow step, Matching. We distinguish them into sort-based, join-based, and unsupervised learning-based methods.

Sort-based Methods.   The core method in this category is *Sorted Neighborhood* (SN) [Hernández and Stolfo, 1995, Puhlmann et al., 2006], which assumes that the lower the lexicographical distance of the blocking keys of two profiles, the more likely they are to match. Thus, SN sorts SB blocking keys in alphabetical order and arranges the associated profiles accordingly. Then, a window of fixed size w slides over the sorted list of profiles and compares the profile at the last position with all other profiles within the same window. SN is very efficient and robust to noise at the end of blocking keys, but depends heavily on w: small w trade high precision (*PQ*) for low recall (*PC*) and vice versa for large w [Christen, 2012b].

Example 3.3   An example of applying the Sorted Neighborhood Blocking with $w = 4$ to the profiles of Figure 2.2 appears in Figure 3.4. As shown in Figure 3.4a, we use the same keys as Standard Blocking in Example 3.2 and Figure 3.3. The keys and the corresponding profiles are

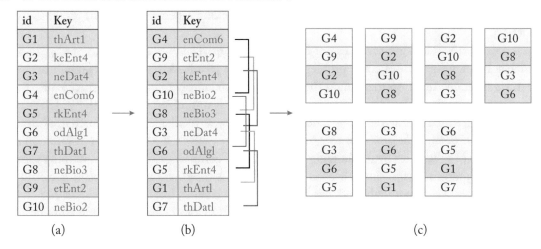

Figure 3.4: Applying *Sorted Neighborhood* with $w = 4$ to the Dirty DS of Figure 2.2 with the Standard Blocking keys of Figure 3.3: (a) the blocking keys of Standard Blocking per profile, (b) the listed of blocking keys sorted in alphabetical order along with the corresponding profile ids, and (c) the final set of blocks.

sorted in alphabetical order in Figure 3.4b. A window of size $w = 4$ slides through the sorted list of profiles to construct the final blocks in Figure 3.4c. In every block, the top profile is compared with all others.

To ameliorate SN's sensitivity to w, *Extended Sorted Neighborhood* [Christen, 2012b, Papadakis et al., 2015] slides a window of fixed size over the sorted list of SB keys—rather than the sorted list of profiles. More advanced methods use a dynamic window, increasing its size if the similarity between the first and the last blocking keys [Ma et al., 2015] or profiles [Yan et al., 2007] exceeds a predetermined threshold. DCS [Draisbach et al., 2012] executes all comparisons within the original window size and increments w by one position at at time, if the average number of duplicates per comparison is higher than a specific threshold ϕ. DCS++ [Draisbach et al., 2012] increases the window size with the next $w - 1$ profiles, even if the ratio between duplicates and comparisons is lower than ϕ; using transitive closure, it skips some windows, saving part of the comparisons.

In a different line of work, *Canopy Clustering* [Christen, 2012b, McCallum et al., 2000] iteratively selects a random profile p_i and creates a new block b_i for it. Using a cheap string similarity measure, it places in b_i all profiles with a similarity to p_i higher than t_{in}; profiles with a similarity higher than $t_{ex} (> t_{in})$ participate in none of the subsequent blocks. *Extended Canopy Clustering* [Christen, 2012b, Papadakis et al., 2015] replaces the weight thresholds with cardinality ones: for each randomly selected profile, the k_1 most similar profiles are placed in its block, while the $k_2(\leq k_1)$ most similar ones participate in no other block. In this way, it ameliorates Canopy Clustering's sensitivity to its weight thresholds, i.e., the fact that high values for t_{in} and, thus, t_{ex} may leave many profiles out of blocks.

Join-based Methods. These techniques leverage string similarity joins (cf. Section 3.3.8) to populate their blocks with nearest neighbors. Schema awareness and domain knowledge is critical in order to define blocking keys that optimize the balance between recall (*PC*) and precision (*PQ*).

Most methods build on *Locality Sensitive Hashing* (LSH), which detects efficiently the pairs of profiles that exceed a similarity threshold, while providing probabilistic guarantees for its effectiveness. LSH is combined with a semantic similarity based on a tree of concepts in Wang et al. [2016b], with Matching in *HARRA* [Kim and Lee, 2010], with K-Means in Steorts et al. [2014] and with an efficient, compact binary Hamming space in Karapiperis et al. [2016] and Karapiperis and Verykios [2016].

On another line of research, blocking keys are mapped to a similarity-preserving Euclidean space of low dimensionality (i.e., between 15 and 25 dimensions). Overlapping blocks are then extracted from this representation through a spatial join. *StringMap* [Christen, 2012b, Jin et al., 2003] uses two weight or cardinality thresholds along with an R-tree or a grid-based index for higher efficiency. The *Double embedding scheme* [Adly, 2009] adds a second Euclidean space of lower dimensionality $d' < d$ and applies a spatial join with a k-d tree to yield the first candidate matches, which are then refined by StringMap.

Unsupervised Learning-based Methods. Due to the lack or scarcity of labeled datasets, these methods rely on automatically generated training instances. *DNF Learner* [Giang, 2015] first applies Matching to a sample of profile pairs, creating a weakly labeled dataset. Based on this dataset, it learns DNF blocking schemes with at most k predicates. Similarly, *FisherDisjunctive* [Kejriwal and Miranker, 2013] considers profile pairs with very low (high) TF-IDF similarity as negative (positive) matches. A Boolean feature vector is associated with every labeled instance, and the discovery of DNF schemes is cast as a Fisher feature selection problem.

3.2.3 HYBRID METHODS

These techniques combine the benefits of local and global functionality.

Sorted Blocks [Draisbach and Naumann, 2011] combines Standard Blocking (SB) with Sorted Neighborhood (SN). First, it sorts all blocking keys and the corresponding profiles in lexicographical order, like SN. Then, it partitions the sorted profiles into disjoint blocks, like SB, using a prefix of the blocking keys. Next, all pairwise comparisons are executed within each block. To avoid missing any matches, an overlap parameter o defines a window of fixed size that includes the o last profiles in the current block together with the first profile of the next block.

The window slides by one position at a time until reaching the oth profile of the next block, executing all pairwise comparisons between profiles from different blocks.

Sorted Blocks is an unconstrained approach that does not restrict block sizes. Thus, it may result in large blocks that dominate its processing time. To address this, two variants set a limit on the maximum block size. *Sorted Blocks New Partition* [Draisbach and Naumann, 2011] creates a new block when the maximum size is reached for a (prefix of) blocking key; the overlap between the blocks ensures that every profile is compared with its predecessors and successors in the sorting order. *Sorted Blocks Sliding Window* [Draisbach and Naumann, 2011] avoids executing all comparisons within a block that is larger than the upper limit; instead, it slides a window equal to the maximum block size over the profiles of the current block.

Finally, *Improved Suffix Arrays Blocking* [de Vries et al., 2009] employs the same blocking keys as Suffix Arrays, but sorts them in alphabetical order, like SN. Then, it compares the consecutive keys with a string similarity measure. If the similarity of two suffixes exceeds a predetermined threshold, the corresponding blocks are merged in an effort to detect duplicates even when there is noise at the end of SB keys, or their sole common key is too frequent. This allows, for example, to detect the high string similarity of the keys "JohnSnith" and "JohnSmith," placing the corresponding profiles into the same block.

3.2.4   DISCUSSION

Regarding the relative performance of Blocking techniques, extensive experimental studies have verified that there is no clear winner among them [Christen, 2012a,b].

As far as running time is concerned, they are all quite efficient, requiring few iterations over the input profiles. However, the global methods are more time-consuming, due to the complexity of their string similarity measures and/or the multiple iterations over the input. The local non-learning methods are faster, as they iterate once over the input, while the run-time of learning-based ones depends on the size of the labeled data.

Regarding effectiveness, they may score an insufficient recall (even $< 50\%$), despite the expert knowledge they leverage. This is especially true for Standard Blocking, Sorted Neighborhood, and their variants that employ a single blocking scheme [Christen, 2012b, Papadakis et al., 2015]. Instead, they should be used in a multi-pass manner with several blocking schemes. In general, their effectiveness depends heavily on parameter configuration, which is typically performed manually. To facilitate this process, *MatchCatcher* [Li et al., 2018] involves a human-in-the-loop functionality that iteratively fine-tunes a blocking method so as to minimize the missed duplicates. Approaches for fully automatic parameter fine-tuning are proposed in Maskat et al. [2016] and O'Hare et al. [2018], while Dalvi et al. [2013] presents an approach to optimizing Blocking for a specific Matching method (e.g., a set of matching rules).

Regardless of their parameter configuration, all blocking methods employ *redundancy* in order to achieve high recall (*PC*). That is, they place every profile into multiple blocks, yielding a set of overlapping blocks that convey two types of unnecessary comparisons [Papadakis et al., 2013, 2015].

1. *Redundant comparisons* occur in multiple blocks, but there is no gain in *PC* by repeating them.

2. *Superfluous comparisons* involve non-matching profiles and, thus, there is no gain in *PC* if we execute them. However, they can only be identified in view of the ground-truth that specifies the correct matches.

3.3   MATCHING

The goal of this step is to derive the resemblance/similarity between all pairs of profiles that have been defined as candidate matches by Blocking, which comprise its input. Its output consists of the set of entities or the *similarity graph*, where every node corresponds to a profile and every pair of compared profiles is connected with an edge, typically weighted in [0, 1] in proportion to their similarity score.

This task has attracted a lot of attention in the literature since the infancy of ER. Yet, it remains an open problem, given that there is no universal approach that achieves high performance under all settings. As a result, more and more complex approaches have been proposed over the years. We distinguish them into seven main categories according to the information they consider when applying a matching function. Their relations are depicted in Figure 3.5. We delve into the distinguishing characteristics and the main methods of each category in the following. Their taxonomy appears in Figure 3.6.

3.3.1   DISTANCE-BASED METHODS

This category involves the simplest Matching methods, which aim to find or develop a string-based distance (or similarity) measure to detect duplicates. Two profiles are considered as duplicates if their assessed distance (similarity) is lower (higher) than a predefined threshold.

The seminal work in Monge and Elkan [1996] tokenizes the textual value of a specific attribute on its special characters (e.g., punctuation), transforming it into a set of "atomic strings." The similarity of two profiles is estimated as the normalized number of matching atomic strings, i.e., atomic strings that are identical or one is the prefix of another.

Inspired from Information Retrieval, *WHIRL* [Cohen, 2000] derives the similarity of two profiles from the cosine similarity between the TF-IDF vectors of specific attribute values. Every dimension corresponds to a distinct token t, with TF standing for its Term Frequency (i.e., the number of times t appears in the value of a specific attribute) and IDF for its Inverse Document Frequency (i.e., the number of profiles that contain t in the specified attribute value).

This approach was extended by *SoftTFIDF* [Bilenko et al., 2003] so that the requirement for identical tokens is relaxed. To support typographical errors, the highly similar tokens are

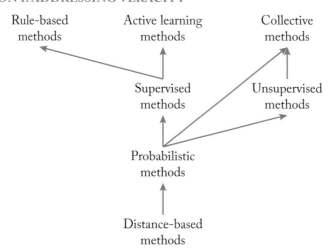

Figure 3.5: The categories of Matching methods and the relation between them. Arrows point from a simpler category to its more complex extension.

also considered as equal. This is done through a secondary character-level measure, such as edit distance, along with an tight threshold.

On another line of research, the overall score for a pair of profiles is estimated as the weighted average of the value similarity for several (aligned) attributes [Dey et al., 1998]. The resulting scores are normalized in $[0, 1]$, while the sum of attribute weights is equal to 1. Fine-tuning them, though, is a challenge.

Multiple attributes are also considered in Guha et al. [2004]. In this case, after comparing the values of candidate matches for n attributes, n ranked lists of profile pairs are produced. To leverage the evidence from all attributes, several efficient approaches are proposed for merging these lists into the top-K best candidate matches.

Discussion.   The main advantage of these approaches is their simplicity and high efficiency that allows them to scale well to large data sources. They also involve a non-learning functionality that requires no labeled instances. However, their effectiveness is limited, because no single similarity measure is suitable for all DSs, as indicated by extensive experimental studies [Cohen et al., 2003]. Even if we know the most suitable measure for the data hand, fine-tuning its *global* threshold that applies uniquely to all profile pairs is non-trivial in practice, typically requiring expert intervention. To ameliorate this requirement, an algorithm that specifies *local* similarity thresholds per profile is proposed in Chaudhuri et al. [2005]—see Section 3.3.5.

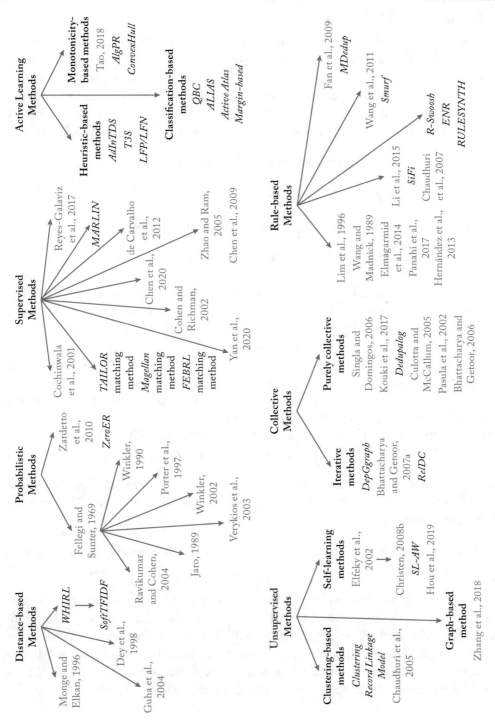

Figure 3.6: The taxonomy of the 1st-generation of Matching methods.

3.3.2 PROBABILISTIC METHODS

The foundations for probabilistic Matching methods were laid in Newcombe et al. [1959] and Newcombe and Kennedy [1962], and were formalized in Fellegi and Sunter [1969]. The resulting framework assumes that every pair of candidate matches, p_i and p_j, is represented by a Boolean vector, where every dimension (i.e., feature) indicates whether p_i agrees or disagrees with p_j on a specific attribute value. It also assumes that every feature is independent of others. Using two cut-off thresholds on the likelihood ratios, it produces three types of decisions:

1. `match` for the pairs that are duplicates with high confidence,

2. `non-match` for the opposite pairs, and

3. `uncertain` for the pairs requiring clerical review by a human expert.

The goal is to optimize these thresholds by minimizing the probability of error through a Bayesian decision model.

This model was combined with an expectation maximization algorithm in Jaro [1989] and with a semi-supervised model in Winkler [2002] for the estimation of probabilities. The Boolean features were replaced by numeric ones in Winkler [1990] and Porter et al. [1997], while the Bayesian decision model was generalized in Verykios et al. [2003]; assuming that the cost of false positive and false negatives is different, it learns decision rules by minimizing of the overall cost. Finally, the original probabilistic approach of Fellegi and Sunter [1969] is generalized in Ravikumar and Cohen [2004] into a hierarchical latent variable graphical model that is suitable for unsupervised learning, taking special care to avoid overfitting.

More practical are the domain-agnostic, fully automatic probabilistic models proposed in Zardetto et al. [2010] and Wu et al. [2020], which rely on two key ideas:

1. the distribution of feature vectors differs among matching and non-matching pairs, which means that the observed vectors are generated by the superposition of two different probability distributions; and

2. the duplicates are rather rare, as their portion in the candidate matches is very low, even after blocking.

In Zardetto et al. [2010], the feature vectors are fitted to a Beta distribution using a pertubation-like approach, and the resulting model is used by a genetic algorithm to cluster the candidate pairs into matches and non-matches. Using multiple similarity functions as features, *ZeroER* [Wu et al., 2020] assumes that the feature vectors are generated by a Gaussian Mixture Model with two mixture components. The model is enhanced with adaptive feature regularization to avoid overfitting and with transitivity to improve its accuracy.

3.3.3   SUPERVISED METHODS

They define Entity Matching as a **binary classification problem**, where the input comprises a pair of profiles and the output is a `match` or `non-match` decision. To solve this problem, they rely on a labeled dataset that involves positive (i.e., matching) and negative (i.e., non-matching) instances (i.e., profile pairs). Every instance is represented by a feature vector, where every dimension typically corresponds to the score returned by a similarity measure, when applied to a specific attribute value. The labeled dataset is partitioned into two disjoint sets: the *training set*, which is used for building the classification model, and the *testing set*, which is used for assessing the classification accuracy.

One of the first supervised approaches leverages classification and regression trees [Cochinwala et al., 2001]. The feature vector consists of the edit distance on specific attribute values and their length in characters. The learned tree is subsequently simplified through pruning, which enhances its generality and robustness.

In Cohen and Richman [2002], a maximum entropy classifier is trained over a set of binary features, such as *EditDistance*(k), which is `true` if the edit distance between two attribute values is lower than $k \in \{0.5, 1, 2, 4, 8, 16, 32, 64\}$. The classifier is applied to all candidate matches, yielding a similarity graph whose edges are weighted by the classification confidence. Greedy agglomerative clustering is then applied to produce the final set of entities.

MARLIN [Bilenko and Mooney, 2003] begins with learning the optimal string similarity measures for the ER task at hand. It uses the Expectation-Maximization algorithm to learn the best cost for the edit distance operations and SVM to learn the best weights in a typical bag (i.e., vector space) model. These measures are then applied to all attribute values of each pair of candidate matches. The resulting feature vector is fed to another SVM classifier that estimates the likelihood that they are duplicates. All candidate matches are sorted according to the classifier's confidence that they are duplicates, and the union-find data structure [Monge and Elkan, 1997] is used for incrementally computing the transitive closure of the detected duplicates.

Two models based on Multilayer Perceptrons with a single hidden layer and a single output node are presented in Reyes-Galaviz et al. [2017]. Each internal node aggregates the scores of a particular similarity measure across all attribute values (Model 1), or the scores of a particular attribute value over all similarity measures (Model 2). The learned weights between the internal and the output nodes indicate the significance of the corresponding similarity measure or attribute value.

In another direction, Matching is cast as a threshold-based ordinal regression task in Yan et al. [2020]. The goal is actually to map profile pairs into one of five categories: `hard-conflict`, `non-conflict`, `weak-match`, `moderate-match`, and `strong-match`. The thresholds corresponding to each category are learned during the training of the regression model. In this way, diverse application settings can be accommodated. For the same reason, the cost function that is minimized can be extended with weights for each type of error.

The above techniques typically represent all attributes with the same features, i.e., they apply the same similarity functions to all textual attribute values. This leads to a larger search space, longer training times, and more complex learned models. To address this issue, a *genetic programming* approach is introduced in de Carvalho et al. [2012]. At its core lies a tree representation of matching rules, where the leaves correspond to attribute values and the internal nodes to operations on them (i.e., similarity functions). A set of genetic operations is iteratively applied to these trees until convergence: *reproduction* retains a tree unchanged, *crossover* extracts two or more new trees from two parent trees, and *mutation* alters an individual tree.

In practice, any classification algorithm can be used for building a supervised matching method. As a result, various classifiers are already implemented by ER tools: ID3 decision trees in *TAILOR* [Elfeky et al., 2002], SVM in *Febrl* [Christen, 2008a], while *Magellan* [Konda et al., 2016] additionally offers naive Bayes, logistic, and linear regression, random forest, and xgboost. In every tool, a series of similarity measures can be used for defining feature vectors, such as Jaccard and Jaro similarity.

However, there is no clear winner among the proposed classification models [Köpcke et al., 2010]. In fact, different classifiers perform better in different contexts. For this reason, some works have focused on combining multiple classification models in order to improve the overall accuracy. Several ensemble learning schemes are empirically explored in Zhao and Ram [2005], such as bagging, boosting, stacking, and cascading. The first two allow for combining classifiers of the same type, while stacking and cascading enable the combination of different models (e.g., decision trees with SVMs), usually outperforming all base classifiers. More principled approaches that rely on meta-level, contextual features are presented in Chen et al. [2009]. These features are combined with the predicted labels of the base classifiers, creating a new labeled dataset that allows for training context-based meta-classifiers.

Finally, on another line of research, a learnable and interpretable framework for risk analysis is proposed in Chen et al. [2020]. Its goal is to rank all labeled instances according to likelihood (risk) of being misclassified by a supervised matching method. To this end, it operates in three steps. First, it represents every labeled instance by the matching rules satisfied by the corresponding pair of profiles. Second, it models the uncertainty of every label by a normal distribution, which is formed by aggregating the matching probability distribution of the individual features. Third, it tunes the parameters of these distributions through a learning-to-rank approach. The end result allows experts to fine-tune the performance of their supervised matching methods based on the high-risk profile pairs.

Discussion.   The supervised methods suffer from the intense **class imbalance** in ER. This issue raises from the fact that the number of duplicates increases linearly with the number of input profiles, while the number of non-matches increases quadratically [Getoor and Machanavajjhala, 2012]. This means that the majority class corresponds to negative instances (i.e., non-matching profile pairs), with the positive ones (duplicate pairs) corresponding to the minority class. To

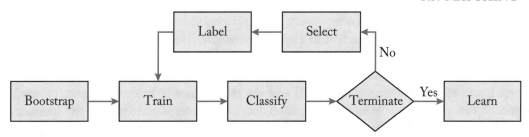

Figure 3.7: The active learning workflow for Entity Resolution.

train an effective classification model, undersampling is typically applied, which randomly samples as many negative instances as the positive ones [Papadakis et al., 2014b].

Another issue faced by supervised methods is the high cost of producing a sufficiently large and representative labeled dataset. Such a dataset usually requires one or more experts, thus being time-consuming and expensive [Wu et al., 2020]. The problem is exacerbated when an extremely large labeled dataset is required. For example, a learning-based industrial system for product matching may need up to 1.5 million labeled instances in order to achieve an F-measure of 99% [Dong and Rekatsinas, 2018]. Hopefully, there are various ways to address this issue:

- transfer learning leverages another, already labeled dataset [Negahban et al., 2012],

- unsupervised learning waives the need for labeled instances altogether (see Section 3.3.5),

- active learning minimizes the number of required labeled instances (see Section 3.3.4), and

- crowdsourcing addresses the challenges of human annotation in a principled manner (see Section 7.2).

Note that active learning differs from crowdsourcing in that a single user, which is usually an expert, is required for manually classifying the selected unlabeled instances [Arasu et al., 2010]. Typically, no monetary cost is incurred. In contrast, crowdsourced techniques involve multiple users and significant monetary cost.

3.3.4   ACTIVE LEARNING METHODS

They minimize the number of labeled instances that are required for learning a robust and effective classification model by implementing the workflow in Figure 3.7.

First, a small set of labeled instances, called *seeds*, is created in order to *bootstrap* the classification model(s). Similar to supervised approaches, each instance corresponds to a pair of profiles and constitutes a feature vector, where every dimension indicates the score returned by a particular similarity measure when applied to a specific attribute. The lack of such labeled instances in the beginning of the process is called *cold-start problem* [Primpeli et al., 2020]. To address it, the seeds are selected randomly [Qian et al., 2017] or based on the distribution of similarity scores [Sarawagi and Bhamidipaty, 2002] and are then manually labeled. A more principled approach that requires no human intervention and no predetermined limit on the number of seeds is presented in Primpeli et al. [2020]. It summarizes the feature vectors into an aggregate similarity score and uses a threshold defined by the elbow point of the score distribution in order to distinguish between matches and non-matches. The instances with the highest confidence are then selected as seeds.

In the second step, the classification model(s) are *trained* over the currently available labeled instances. Next, all unlabeled instances are classified by the trained model(s). A *termination criterion* is then evaluated. This might be as simple as reaching a maximum number of iterations/manually labeled instances, or as complex as converging to an estimated performance target over the unlabeled instances [Meduri et al., 2020]. When this criterion is satisfied, a supervised approach is applied to *learn* a (set of) classification model(s) over the final set of labeled instances. Otherwise, the active learning process continues with the *select* step, which identifies the most ambiguous unlabeled instances. These are the instances that are harder to be classified, i.e., they correspond to the minimum confidence of the trained model(s). The selected instances are *manually labeled* and then the *train* step is repeated.

The most crucial step in the active learning workflow is *select*, due to the intense class imbalance in ER. Using random sampling in this step would yield a set of instances that are dominated by non-matching pairs of profiles. Moreover, the quality of the final classification models depends on the representativity and informativeness of the instances that are manually labeled. Therefore, sophisticated algorithms are required for this step. Several methods have been proposed in the literature. We distinguish them into the following three categories.

Heuristic-based methods.   They select ambiguous unlabeled instances judging from their feature vectors.

AdInTDS [Christen et al., 2015] recursively partitions the set of unlabeled instances into subsets that are considered pure, i.e., they presumably involve only matches or non-matches. The most representative instances are then selected from each cluster for manual annotation.

T3S [Bianco et al., 2015] is carried out in two steps: first, the similarity scores of the unlabeled instances are discretized,[2] and a balanced set of instances is randomly selected from each bin. Second, the original instances are cleaned from the redundant ones (i.e., those with very similar feature vectors), yielding a smaller set that includes the most dissimilar (i.e., most informative) instances to be labeled.

LFP/LFN [Qian et al., 2017] is crafted for learning ER rules in disjunctive normal form. The LFP phase raises precision by selecting likely false positives, i.e., unlabeled instances that

---

[2]For example, the [0, 1] domain of similarity scores is split into 10 bins: $[0, 0.1), [0.1, 02), \ldots, [0.9, 1.0]$.

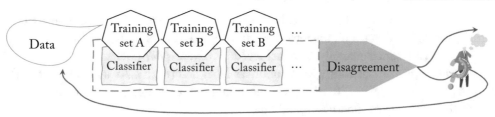

Figure 3.8: Outline of the *query-by-committee* (QBC) approach to active learning.

are predicted as matches by the current rules, but are likely to be non-matches according to a feature similarity heuristic. The LFN phase raises recall by selecting likely false negatives, i.e., unlabeled instances that are predicted as non-matches by the current rules, but are likely to be matches.

Classification-based methods.   They select ambiguous unlabeled instances according to the confidence of the models trained over the current training set.

In the *query-by-committee* (QBC) strategy, which is outlined in Figure 3.8, a set of classifiers is trained and the ambiguous instances are selected according to the disagreement of their predictions, as it is quantified by entropy or variance [Meduri et al., 2020, Mozafari et al., 2014]. *ALIAS* [Sarawagi and Bhamidipaty, 2002] uses homogeneous sets of classifiers (Decision Trees, SVM, or Naive Bayes), with every classifier learned with different (randomized) parameters, from a different sample of the training set or from a different subset of features. A committee of decision trees is also used by *Active Atlas* [Tejada et al., 2002]. A natural approach is offered by random forests, with their individual trees acting as the classifier committee [Meduri et al., 2020]. QBC was generalized in Mozafari et al. [2014] into a learner-agnostic strategy that can be combined with any classifier, be it linear, non-convex nonlinear, tree-based or rule-based.

In the *margin-based* strategy, the most ambiguous instances are those closer to the classifiers' decision boundary, i.e., 0.5 classification probability for nonlinear classifiers like neural networks, or the separating hyperplane of linear classifiers [Meduri et al., 2020, Mozafari et al., 2014].

Monotonicity-based methods.   They learn a model that maximizes recall under a user-determined precision constraint, offering probabilistic guarantees on their performance, unlike the methods of the other categories. They rely on the monotonicity of precision, which dictates that if two profiles are matching, then any pair of profiles with greater or equal similarity in all considered features is also considered as a match [Tao, 2018]. Hence, the precision of a matching rule $sim(p_i, p_j) > \theta$ can be safely considered as a monotonically increasing function of the similarity threshold θ.

Using N similarity functions on specific attributes as features, *AlgPR* [Arasu et al., 2010] defines an N-dimensional feature space and performs a binary search over this space to identify the most ambiguous unlabeled instances. In the worst case, though, its label complexity is linear, requiring manual labeling for all unlabeled instances [Bellare et al., 2013].

Better performance guarantees are achieved by *ConvexHull* [Bellare et al., 2013], which learns a Pareto-optimal classifier with a sublinear label complexity. At its core lies the IWAL algorithm [Beygelzimer et al., 2010], which selects ambiguous instances in a way that guarantees matching the error rate of supervised methods.

Finally, several algorithms with performance guarantees are presented in Tao [2018], optimizing the balance between the cost (i.e., number of labeled instances) and the accuracy of the learned classifier.

Discussion. The performance of active learning techniques is evaluated with respect to the common effectiveness measures (Precision, Recall, and F-Measure) as well as in terms of three specialized measures [Meduri et al., 2020]:

1. the number of instances that were manually labeled—the fewer they are, the more effective is the active learning approach;

2. interpretability, which assesses how intelligible the final classification model is; usually, the simpler it is (e.g., by involving fewer rules), the better; and

3. the latency of the overall process, i.e., the time required for the select, label, train, and classify steps.

Note that to reduce latency, blocking can be used to clean the pool of unlabeled instances from obvious non-matches [Arasu et al., 2010, Meduri et al., 2020], while the classify step could apply incremental learning to enrich the already trained models with newly labeled instances [Meduri et al., 2020].

A comprehensive experimental analysis of the main methods is presented in Meduri et al. [2020]. A interesting finding is that using random forests as QBC typically yields an effectiveness that is equivalent or even better than supervised models that require orders of magnitude more labeled instances.

3.3.5   UNSUPERVISED METHODS

One of the first unsupervised methods was proposed in Monge and Elkan [1997]. Assuming that transitivity among duplicates holds, it represents every entity by one of its profiles. A priority queue Q maintains all detected entities, sorted in lexicographical order. Starting from the top of Q, every input profile p_i is compared with every entity $e_k \in Q$ by applying the Smith–Waterman similarity measure to p_i and the representative profile of e_k, which is determined through the function $Q.Find(e_k)$. If their similarity exceeds a predetermined threshold, p_i is merged with e_k through the function $Q.Union(p_i, e_k)$, which also updates the representative of e_k. If p_i is not merged with any entity in Q, it creates a new one that is placed into Q. The entire processing is repeated using the reverse lexicographical order of entities.

Most subsequent unsupervised methods use the same representation as the supervised techniques: every pair of profiles is represented by a feature vector, where every dimension corresponds to the similarity score for a particular attribute value. Yet, they are more generic than supervised techniques, as they are independent of a labeled dataset with positive and negative instances. Instead, they learn a matching model in one of the following three ways.

Clustering-based methods.   The earliest one is *Clustering Record Linkage Model* [Elfeky et al., 2002]. Essentially, it applies k-means clustering to the feature vectors of the candidate matches, with $k = 3$, assuming that all similarity scores are normalized to $[0, 1]$, with 1 (0) denoting equivalence (dissimilarity). The cluster with its center closer to $[0, 0, \ldots, 0]$ encompasses the non-matches, the one with its center closer to $[1, 1, \ldots, 1]$ conveys the duplicate pairs, and the remaining one involves the potential matches that require clerical review.

A different clustering approach is proposed in Chaudhuri et al. [2005]. First, it computes the nearest neighbors of each input profile. Then, it partitions the input profiles into *valid* entities, which satisfy two criteria: (i) they form compact sets, as it assumed that duplicates are mutually nearest neighbors; **and** (ii) they have sparse neighborhoods, as it assumed that duplicates are far from other, non-matching profiles. These two criteria, which can be combined with any similarity measure(s), overcome the need for a global threshold.

Self-learning methods.   They leverage a weakly labeled dataset, which identifies as positive the instances with a similarity higher than a predetermined threshold t_h and as negative the instances with a similarity lower than another threshold t_l ($t_l \ll t_h$). The resulting seed instances are then used for training a supervised model. This idea was introduced in Elfeky et al. [2002] and was improved in Christen [2008b], which replaced the threshold-based seed selection with a nearest neighbor search and used an incrementally trained SVM for classification.

SL-AW [Jurek et al., 2017] learns an ensemble of self-learning models, where each model employs a different set of similarity measures/features. During seed selection, the features are weighted in proportion to their distinctiveness, while special care is taken to select seeds with high diversity. The contribution of each model is then assessed and those performing poorly are discarded.

In Hou et al. [2019], self-learning is generalized to *gradual machine learning*, where the seed instances are used to learn a classification model that is iteratively extended to classify more challenging unlabeled instances. This approach is inspired from the cognitive process in humans, who start with learning easy tasks and gradually continue with more complex tasks.

Graph-based methods.   A graph-theoretic approach is presented in Zhang et al. [2018]. Based on the idea that duplicates share distinctive attribute value tokens, the first phase, called *ITER*, builds a weighted bipartite graph that connects these tokens with profile pairs. ITER starts with random weights and converges to a similarity score for each pair through a recursive procedure that is similar to PageRank [Brin and Page, 1998]. The second phase, called *CliqueRank*, builds a graph, where the nodes correspond to individual profiles and the edges connect the pairs with at least one common token, weighted with the similarity scores computed by ITER. A random walk process then estimates the matching probability for each pair.

3.3.6   COLLECTIVE METHODS

All the above approaches classify every pair of profiles, p_i and p_j, independently of the others, i.e., the match decision considers exclusively the evidence retrieved when applying similarity measures on the attribute values of p_i and p_j. In contrast, *collective methods* rely on the idea that all match decisions are interrelated—not only when it comes to profiles of the same type, but also for profiles of different types. This notion is typically illustrated through examples from the bibliography domain: identifying two authors as duplicates increases the likelihood that their similar co-authors are also matching (profiles of the same type) as well as the likelihood that venues or publications with similar titles are also duplicates (profiles of different type).

Collective methods are distinguished into two types [Rastogi et al., 2011].

1. The *iterative* methods process a set of candidate matches repetitively, using the new matches to update the matching likelihood of the related profiles. They typically rely on a graph that models the dependencies and/or the relations between the given profiles.

2. The *purely collective* methods typically employ sophisticated probabilistic models that capture the relations between the given profiles and take holistic (i.e., global) match decisions.

Both types combine attribute similarities with contextual (relational) information, but the latter type typically involves a higher computational cost [Kouki et al., 2017].

Iterative methods.   They were pioneered by *DepGgraph* [Dong et al., 2005], where every graph node corresponds to a pair of profiles (i.e., candidate matches), while the edges connect pairs whose similarities are interrelated. A priority queue contains all nodes to be processed, and in every iteration, the top node is removed and evaluated; if the similarity of two profiles exceeds a predetermined threshold, they are merged, the graph model is updated accordingly, and their neighboring nodes are placed in the priority queue.

A similar greedy algorithm is proposed in Bhattacharya and Getoor [2007a], where the nodes of the graph model correspond to profiles and the edges connect the related ones, with hyper-edges connecting multiple related nodes (e.g., more than two authors in a publication). The contextual similarity of two nodes is determined by their connectivity as well as the connectivity of their neighbors using various relational measures.

The graph model of *RelDC* [Kalashnikov and Mehrotra, 2006] involves two types of nodes: (i) the regular ones, which correspond to profiles (e.g., authors); and (ii) the choice ones, which connect a regular node with two or more regular nodes that are its candidate matches. The regular nodes are connected with each other with unweighted edges, as determined by their relations (e.g., co-authors), and with weighted edges to the choice nodes. The goal is to estimate these weights iteratively, combining the attribute similarities with contextual evidence

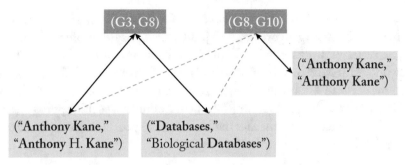

Figure 3.9: Applying *DepGgraph* to the Dirty DS of Figure 2.2.

from the path length between candidate matches—longer paths yield lower weights and, thus, lower matching likelihood.

Example 3.4 Collective methods focus on enriching the profile information in each iteration. Applied to the profiles of Figure 2.2, *DepGgraph* initially computes the similarity of G3 with G8, given the resemblance between the record names, affiliation, etc. Figure 3.9 shows part of the graph generated by *DepGgraph*. This results in merging G3 with G8. The merging implies that all information of G3 and G8 can now be used by both records, as shown with dashed lines in the figure. Thus, the following iteration will use *City, University of London* as the affiliation of G8 and not *unknown* as in the original record. This will increase the belief for merging G8 with G10.

Purely collective methods. They differ in the statistical relational model that captures the contextual information and infers the match decisions.

In Singla and Domingos [2006], Markov Logic Networks (MLNs) are used to specify a set of *soft constraints*, i.e., matching rules that are weighted according to their importance, and to find the joint match decisions that minimize the aggregate weight of violated rules.

A similar optimization problem is solved in Kouki et al. [2017] in the context of familial networks using Probabilistic Soft Logic. This approach supports matching rules that involve predicates with numeric truth values (in [0, 1])—unlike MLNs, which exclusively support Boolean predicates.

Dedupalog [Arasu et al., 2009] offers a declarative, domain-agnostic language for specifying soft and *hard constraints* (i.e., matching rules that cannot be violated). After modeling the task at hand with this language, the system applies an approximately optimal, graph-based algorithm similar to Correlation Clustering to minimize the number of violated soft constraints, while respecting all hard constraints.

In Culotta and McCallum [2005], *Conditional Random Fields* are combined with a relational agglomerative clustering algorithm that jointly deduplicates profiles.

Finally, a series of works employ Dirichlet process mixture models, such as relational Bayesian networks with Markov Chain Monte Carlo in Pasula et al. [2002] and Latent Dirichlet Allocation model with Gibbs sampling in Bhattacharya and Getoor [2006]. These models are extended in Bhattacharya and Getoor [2006] with domain-specific approaches that capture cross-attribute dependencies (e.g., the fact that each venue specializes in a specific research field, thus publishing works with similar titles).

3.3.7   RULE-BASED METHODS

The main disadvantage of supervised methods is their limited interpretability: their decisions are unclear even to experts, when using complex classifiers like SVMs. Yet, interpretability is crucial for a number of tasks on ER solutions, such as maintenance, debugging, execution optimization, and integration of domain knowledge [Singh et al., 2017]. To address this issue, early supervised methods convert a trained classifier like a decision tree into a set of rules [Tejada et al., 2001]. Better results can be derived from specialized techniques that directly create matching rules.

In more detail, a **matching rule** typically takes the form $X \Rightarrow Y$, where X is a set of predicates on specific attributes of an individual profile or a pair of profiles, and Y corresponds to an entity or a decision that is binary (`match` or `non-match`) or ternary, including `uncertain` as the third option that calls for clerical review [Christen, 2012a]. X is the left-hand side (LHS) and Y the right-hand side (RHS) of the rule [Koumarelas et al., 2020, Li et al., 2015]. X usually comes in Dinjunctive or Conjunctive Normal Form [Christen, 2012a, Panahi et al., 2017], with predicates of the form $p_i.attr_k \ op \ p_j.attr_k$ or $p_j.attr_k \ op \ value$, where p_l stands for a profile, $attr_k$ for an attribute value in p_l and $value$ for a hard-coded attribute value, while the operator is $op \in \{=, <, >, \leq, \geq\}$. Alternatively, the predicates are of the form $sim(p_i.attr_k, p_j.attr_k) \geq \theta$ or $sim(p_j.attr_k, value) \geq \theta$, where sim is a similarity function and θ a similarity threshold. Each rule might be associated with a weight that designates the confidence in its correctness [Li et al., 2015].

Note that the matching rules are distinguished into *positive* and *negative* ones, with the latter involving at least one predicate that uses negation. The matching rules are further distinguished according to their granularity into *attribute-matching* and *record-matching* ones; the former involve a single predicate in its LHS, while the latter constitute a set of attribute-matching rules [Wang et al., 2011].

The effectiveness of matching rules is assessed by two measures [Christen, 2012a].

1. *Accuracy*, similar to precision, expresses the portion of the profiles or profile pairs that satisfy LHS that also satisfy RHS.

2. *Coverage*, similar to recall, expresses the portion of profiles or profile pairs that satisfy LHS among all input data.

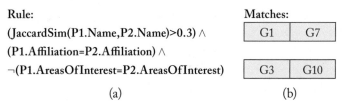

Figure 3.10: Applying a matching rule to the Dirty DS of Figure 2.2: (a) the matching rule and (b) the set of detected entities.

Both measures are defined in [0, 1], with higher values indicating higher effectiveness. However, there is a trade-off between them [Christen, 2012a]: to achieve high accuracy, a matching rule usually needs to be very specific, thus restricting its coverage, and vice versa. To address this trade-off, the rule-based algorithms typically achieve high coverage by producing a set of highly accurate matching rules [Li et al., 2015, Singh et al., 2017].

Example 3.5   Figure 3.10 illustrates a simple example of applying a matching rule to the Dirty DS of Figure 2.2. Figure 3.10a presents the set of predicates constructing the rule. The first predicate makes use of the Jaccard similarity for the "Name" attribute of two profiles with threshold $\theta = 0.3$. The second predicate requires that the values of "Affiliation" attribute should be identical for the two compared profiles. Finally, the third predicate requires that the values of "Areas of Interest" must be different. The last predicate is a negation and thus renders the matching rule negative. Figure 3.10b demonstrates the profile pairs that are detected as duplicates by this matching rule.

Some rule-based approaches solicit matching rules from experts, leveraging their domain knowledge. The experts actually combine the values of several attributes to extract from each profile a key that facilitates the detection of duplicates [Lim et al., 1996, Wang and Madnick, 1989]. More recent approaches develop interactive systems [Elmagarmid et al., 2014, Panahi et al., 2017] or scripting languages [Hernández et al., 2013] that allow for defining and testing matching rules. Given that these manual processes are time-consuming and error-prone [Singh et al., 2017], most algorithms involve a hybrid approach that enables domain experts to refine and debug a set of rules that were automatically learned [Elmagarmid et al., 2007] or learn matching rules in a fully automatic way. The latter approach typically involves two steps [Li et al., 2015]: (i) the learning phase and (ii) the application phase.

Methods for Learning Matching Rules.   The learning phase leverages a labeled set of positive and negative instances (i.e., pairs of matching and non-matching profiles, respectively) to efficiently discover a set of matching rules that achieve high accuracy and high coverage. Constraints are usually considered in order to avoid overfitting and ensure the high time efficiency of the next phase.

In Li et al. [2015], each rule contains up to l predicates (*length constraint*), and there should be no redundancy between the resulting rules (*minimality constraint*).

The latter problem is also addressed by SiFi [Wang et al., 2011], which eliminates two types of redundancy.

1. *Threshold redundancy*, where two rules r_1 and r_2 differ only in their similarity thresholds such that $\theta_1 > \theta_2$, and the results of r_2 differ from those of r_1 only in positive instances.

2. *Similarity function redundancy*, where two rules r_1 and r_2 use different similarity functions and thresholds and the positive instances that are correctly classified by r_1 are a subset of those correctly classified by r_2, while the negative instances that are correctly identified by r_2 are a subset of those correctly identified by r_1.

In both cases, r_1 is redundant with respect to r_2. A similar task was also addressed in Chaudhuri et al. [2007], but for a limited set of similarity functions.

Methods for Applying Matching Rules.   The application of matching rules depends on the type of operators they involve.

In *exact-match rules*, all predicates use the operator $=$ and can be efficiently carried out by checking the equivalence of attribute values [Wang et al., 2011].

More frequent are the *approximate-match rules*, which involve similarity functions and thresholds, thus requiring specialized similarity join techniques for their efficient computation [Koumarelas et al., 2020, Wang et al., 2011]. Techniques for accelerating the execution of rules with a single predicate are described in Section 3.3.8, whereas rules with multiple predicates can be accelerated by *Smurf* [C. et al., 2018]. Assuming that such complex matching rules can be represented as Random Forests, Smurf reuses computations across the trees to speed up their execution.

Generic algorithms for applying matching (and merging) rules are proposed in Benjelloun et al. [2009] and Whang et al. [2009a]. Both works treat the matching and merging rules as black boxes and apply them in the optimal way based on the ICAR properties, i.e., idempotence, commutativity, associativity, and representativity. They differ, though, in the type of rules they support.

R-Swoosh [Benjelloun et al., 2009] is crafted for positive rules and operates as follows: initially, it places all input profiles into a queue Q, while an empty list E contains all entities identified so far. The first profile p_1 is iteratively removed from Q and is compared with all entities in E. If p_1 matches with no entity, it is simply added in E. If p_1 matches with $e_j \in E$,

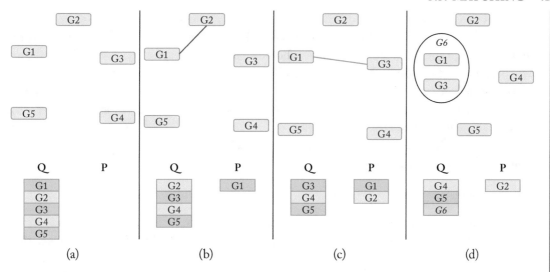

Figure 3.11: R-swoosh functionality.

then they are merged and the result is placed into Q, while e_j is removed form E. This process is repeated until Q is empty.

Example 3.6 Figure 3.11 illustrates a simple example of the R-Swoosh algorithm functionality. List P is initially empty in Figure 3.11a and Profile G1 is the first to be added. Profile G2 is compared with G1 in Figure 3.11b without obtaining a match and it is therefore also added to P. Profile G3 is the next to be processed and it is matched with G1 in Figure 3.11c. The two profiles are merged into a new Profile G6 which is put back to queue Q, while G1 and G3 are deleted, as shown in Figure 3.11d.

ENR [Whang et al., 2009a] is crafted for unary and binary negative rules; the former check whether a profile is valid in itself, while the latter check whether two profiles are consistent so that they can coexist in the ER outcome. *ENR* applies these rules proactively, resolving the inconsistencies that arise through four strategies: (i) discard data, which excludes one of the inconsistent profiles from the end result; (ii) forced merge, where an expert merges manually two inconsistent profiles; (iii) override rule, where an expert manually determines that a negative rule was falsely activated; and (iv) a combination of these strategies.

Recently, a more flexible and concise form of matching rules was proposed in Singh et al. [2017]. They are derived from the *general Boolean formula* and are equivalent to if-then-else rules. Despite the large search space that results from their high expressivity, *RULESYNTH* [Singh et al., 2017] learns them efficiently from a small set of positive and negative labeled instances.

Another form of advanced matching rules are the *matching dependencies* (MDs) [Fan et al., 2009]; they are generalizations of functional dependencies, declaring that if some attributes match, then some other attributes should match, too [Fan et al., 2009]. As an example, consider the following bibliographical MD: `sim(title)>0.75 ∧ sim(venue)>0.9 →` `sim(authors)>0.8`. Reasoning algorithms for deducing more MDs from a set of given MDs are proposed in Fan et al. [2009], while *MDedup* [Koumarelas et al., 2020] learns a regression model that is able to predict the effectiveness of arbitrary sets of MDs. The model is trained on a set of minimal MDs that are automatically extracted from DSs with ground-truth and can be applied to DSs without ground-truth.

3.3.8   STRING SIMILARITY JOINS

These techniques are mainly used for detecting near duplicate documents [Bayardo et al., 2007], but they are also widely used for accelerating the execution of Matching. In essence, they identify rapidly and discard candidate matches that do not satisfy matching rules of the form $sim(v_i, v_j) > \theta$, where *sim* stands for a similarity measure, v_k for the string value of a specific attribute in profile p_k, and θ for the minimum similarity threshold for duplicates, usually in $(0, 1)$ [Augsten and Böhlen, 2013]. As an example, consider the following matching rule for movies: JaccardSim(title$_1$,title$_2$) > 0.8.

Depending on the granularity of the similarity measure, we distinguish string similarity joins into two categories [Augsten and Böhlen, 2013, Jiang et al., 2014]:

1. the *character-based methods* compare v_i with v_j by representing them as sequences of characters, using (a variation of) edit distance to compute the minimum character transformations required to convert v_i into v_j; and

2. the *token-based methods* transform v_i and v_j into sets through tokenization or q-gram extraction and then, compare the sets using a set-based similarity measure like Overlap, Jaccard, Cosine, or Dice.

In practice, a matching rule can be equivalently expressed in any similarity measure through appropriate transformations [Augsten and Böhlen, 2013, Jiang et al., 2014]: a similarity threshold θ on any similarity measure can be transformed into an equivalent Overlap threshold τ that depends on the size of the sets, as explained in Figure 3.12.

In a nutshell, the similarity join techniques *a priori* discard the vast majority of candidate matches that do not satisfy a given matching rule in an efficient way. Thus, they lower the runtime of Matching without any cost in recall, providing an *exact solution* that misses no duplicates. To this end, they usually operate in two steps that form the *Filter-Verification framework* [Augsten and Böhlen, 2013]:

1. *Filtering* sweeps the obvious non-matches away, without applying the similarity measure, and

Type of Joins	Measure	Definition	Equivalent Overlap Threshold
Character-based	Edit distance	# character transformations	$\max(|x|, |y|) + 1 - (1 + \theta) \times q$
Token-based	Overlap	$|\mathbf{x} \cap \mathbf{y}|$	θ
	Cosine	$|\mathbf{x} \cap \mathbf{y}|/\sqrt{|x| \cdot |y|}$	$\theta \times \sqrt{|x| \cdot |y|}$
	Dice	$2 \cdot |\mathbf{x} \cap \mathbf{y}|/(|x| + |y|)$	$\theta \times (|x| + |y|)/2$
	Jaccard	$|\mathbf{x} \cap \mathbf{y}|/|x| + |y| - |\mathbf{x} \cap \mathbf{y}|$	$\theta \times (|x| + |y|)/(1 + \theta)$

Figure 3.12: Definition of the main similarity measures used by string similarity joins, along with formulas for transforming a threshold θ into an equivalent Overlap threshold.

2. *Verification* cleans the remaining candidate matches from the false positives.

Given that Verification merely executes the matching rule, research focuses exclusively on Filtering.

Most filtering techniques extract signatures from v_i and v_j such that they satisfy the matching rule if their signatures overlap [Augsten and Böhlen, 2013, Jiang et al., 2014, Mann et al., 2016]. An inverted index is then constructed over the signatures so that the candidate matches are generated efficiently. The main index-based filtering techniques are the following (where possible, we present their form when applied in combination with a Jaccard similarity threshold θ).

- *Length Filtering* [Gravano et al., 2001] states that two values are similar only if their lengths are within certain bounds. In our example, Length Filtering takes the following form: $|v_j| \cdot \theta \leq |v_i| \leq |v_j|/\theta$.

- *Count Filtering* [Gravano et al., 2001] demands that v_i's signature shares at least τ elements with that of v_j. In our example, $\tau = \lceil \theta \cdot |v_j| \rceil$.

- *Prefix Filtering* [Bayardo et al., 2007, Chaudhuri et al., 2006] transforms every value into a set and sorts its elements in increasing order of frequency across the entire DS(s). Then, it creates a π-prefix with the π least frequent elements and states that v_i and v_j are similar if their π-prefixes share at least one element. The prefix size π differs for each value and depends on the selected similarity measure and threshold. In our example, $\pi(v_j) = \lfloor (1 - \theta) \cdot |v_j| \rfloor + 1$.

- Prefix Filtering is enhanced in various ways: *Positional Filtering* [Xiao et al., 2008] performs a stricter pruning by considering the actual positions of the common elements in the prefixes of v_i and v_j; *Group Filtering* [Bouros et al., 2012] clusters together values with identical prefixes, treating them as a single set during candidate generation. In this way, it probes less times into the inverted list. Grouped values are unfolded during verification; *Adaptive Prefix Filtering* [Wang et al., 2012b] optimizes dynamically the

	Length filtering	Count filtering	Prefix filtering	Positional filtering	Suffix filtering	Adaptive filtering	Partition filtering	Triangle inequality
PassJoin							✓	
AllPairs	✓		✓					
PPJoin	✓		✓	✓				
PPJoin+	✓		✓	✓	✓			
GroupJoin	✓		✓	✓				
AdaptJoin	✓					✓		
LIMES								✓

Figure 3.13: The filtering techniques used by the main string similarity join algorithms.

prefix length for each value; and *Suffix Filtering* [Xiao et al., 2008] applies a divide-and-conquer strategy that calculates the maximum possible number of elements shared by the suffixes of v_i and v_j, i.e., in the rest of their signatures after excluding their prefixes.

• Based on the pigeonhole principle, *Partition Filtering* [Li et al., 2011] splits v_i and v_j into multiple segments such that they satisfy the similarity condition if they have at least one segment in common. This constraint is strengthened by the *pigeonring principle* [Qin and Xiao, 2018], which additionally considers the order of segments.

• The *Triangle Inequality Filtering* [Ngomo and Auer, 2011] skips a pairwise comparison by estimating lower and upper bounds of the distance between two values based on their precomputed distances from specific reference values, called *exemplars*. It is suitable only for metric spaces (e.g., edit distance and Euclidean distance for numbers and vectors).

Combinations and adaptations of these techniques lay the ground for various string similarity join algorithms, as shown in Figure 3.13. We observe that Length and Prefix Filtering lie at the core of most algorithms, followed by Positional Filtering.

In another line of research, recent methods replace the inverted indices with *tree-based* ones, like tries [Wang et al., 2010] and B$^+$-trees [Zhang et al., 2017b, 2010]. These accelerate primarily character-based joins. Other approaches offer an *approximate filtering* that favors time efficiency and high scalability over completeness: they relax the requirement for not missing any duplicates in order to achieve even lower runtimes. They convert the attribute values into a low-dimensional representation and use hashing techniques, predominantly LSH, such that the similar ones are more likely to be mapped to the same bucket than dissimilar ones. Probabilistic guarantees are usually provided for the quality of the end result [Satuluri and Parthasarathy, 2012, Tao et al., 2009].

Discussion.   The relative performance of similarity join techniques has been thoroughly examined in two recent experimental analyses [Jiang et al., 2014, Mann et al., 2016]. Among the character-based methods, Partition Filtering gives rise to the most efficient approach (i.e., PassJoin [Li et al., 2011]), which minimizes the number of segments that are required to find candidate matches [Jiang et al., 2014]; for short strings, though, FastSS [Thomas Bocek, 2007] works even faster [Jiang et al., 2014].

For the token/set-based methods, the length of strings has no significant impact on efficiency—they are capable of processing both short value attribute values and long texts like a Web page [Bayardo et al., 2007, Xiao et al., 2008]. More important is the role of similarity threshold. For example, the higher the Jaccard similarity threshold is, the deeper is the pruning performed by Prefix Filtering. In general, though, the top performing method depends on the cost of Verification [Mann et al., 2016]: the lower it is, the simpler filtering techniques should be preferred. In other words, complex Filtering does not pay off when the verification cost is minimized. In these settings, plain Prefix Filtering (i.e., AllPairs [Bayardo et al., 2007]) is typically the best choice, while its combination with positional (i.e., PPJoin [Xiao et al., 2008]) and Group Filtering (i.e., GroupJoin [Bouros et al., 2012]) achieves the best median and average performance, respectively, [Mann et al., 2016]. For costly Verification, the best performance is achieved by Adaptive Prefix Filtering (i.e., AdaptJoin [Wang et al., 2012b]) as well as the combination of Prefix, Positional and Suffix Filtering (i.e., PPJoin+ [Xiao et al., 2008]).

3.4   CLUSTERING

This optional step produces the final set of entities from the *similarity graph* it receives as input. Most relevant techniques involve an unsupervised functionality that is *partitional* (i.e., it produces disjoint sets of profiles) and *unconstrained*, as it does not require the number of **equivalence clusters** (i.e., final entities) as input [Hassanzadeh et al., 2009]. We distinguish them according to the ER task they target, since only the methods presented in Betancourt et al. [2016] apply uniformly to all types of ER—based on the *microclustering property*, they ensure that the number of profiles in each entity grows sublinearly with the size of the input data.

Methods for Clean-Clean ER.   Their similarity graph is bipartite, albeit unbalanced. Based on the 1-1 correspondence of duplicates between the two input DSs, they match each node/profile from the one vertex set with the most similar one from the other vertex set. This task can be carried out by the *Hungarian algorithm* [Kuhn, 1955], preferably through an approximation that lowers its computational cost (e.g., [Díaz and Fernández, 2001, Kurtzberg, 1962]). An alternative is the *stable marriage* algorithm for unequal sets [McVitie and Wilson, 1970], also called *Unique Mapping Clustering* [Lacoste-Julien et al., 2013], which operates as follows: first, it sorts all edges in decreasing weight and then, it iteratively considers the profiles of the top edge as duplicates, if its weight exceeds a predetermined threshold and none of the adjacent nodes/profiles has already been matched.

Methods for Dirty ER.   The simplest approach is *Connected Components* [Hassanzadeh et al., 2009, Saeedi et al., 2018a], which first applies a cut-off threshold and then estimates the transitive closure of the remaining edges. This approach is quite efficient, iterating once over all edges, but is rather sensitive to noise.

To address this issue, more elaborate algorithms build more robust clusters around selected nodes, which operate as centers. *Center Clustering* [Haveliwala et al., 2000] defines as centers the nodes with the highest average weight, while *Merge-Center Clustering* [Hassanzadeh and Miller, 2009] extends it to unite clusters with centers similar to the same node. *Star Clustering* [Aslam et al., 2004] promotes the nodes with the highest degree and is enhanced by *Ricochet Clustering* [Wijaya and Bressan, 2009], which (re-)assigns nodes to their closer cluster centers, similar to K-Means. The *Fusion* framework [Yan et al., 2020] partitions each connected component into smaller clusters so as to resolve conflicts between its profiles. The same is done by *Global Edge Consistency Gain* [Draisbach et al., 2020], which iteratively changes an edge from `non-match` (i.e., with a weight below a given threshold) to `match`, and vice versa, as long as the overall consistency gets higher—that is, the number of triangles with no, one or all edges marked as `match` increases.

Example 3.7   Figure 3.14 illustrates the steps of applying Center Clustering to a similarity graph derived from the DS of Figure 2.2. The edges are processed in decreasing order of weight, i.e., similarity score. Therefore, $< G2, G5 >$ and $< G8, G10 >$ are the first edges to be processed in Figure 3.14b. In Figure 3.14c, node G2 is set as the center node and G5 as the non-center one, because the former has an average weight of $0.9/1 = 0.9$ and the latter an average weight of $(0.6 + 0.9)/2 = 0.75$. When the nodes of the processed edge are not yet labeled and have the same average weight, one of them is randomly labeled as center node, e.g., node G1 when the processing edge $< G1, G7 >$ in Figure 3.14d. When the edge to be processed connects a center node with a non-labeled one, the latter is labeled as non-center, e.g., node G3 when processing edge $< G10, G3 >$ in Figure 3.14e. When the edge to be processed connects a non-center node with a non-labeled one or two nodes with the same label, no action is performed, as shown for edges $< G3, G8 >$ and $< G5, G9 >$ in Figure 3.14f. The resulting equivalence clusters, i.e., entities, are illustrated in Figure 3.15.

More advanced techniques amplify the strength of *intra-links*, i.e., the edges inside each cluster, while abating the strength of *inter-cluster links*, i.e., the edges across different clusters. To this end, *Markov Clustering* [Van Dongen, 2000] relies on random walks, *Cut clustering* [Flake et al., 2003] leverages the minimum cuts of maximum flow paths, whereas *Correlation Clustering* [Bansal et al., 2004] solves an NP-hard optimization problem, relying on approximations for higher efficiency [Kushagra et al., 2019]. A detailed experimental analysis demonstrates that Markov Clustering consistently achieves the top performance among these methods [Hassanzadeh et al., 2009].

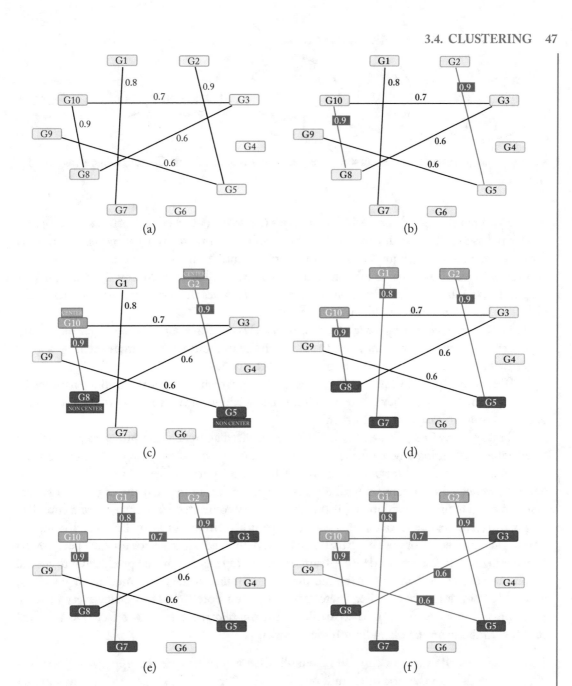

Figure 3.14: An example of Center Clustering: (a) a similarity graph derived from the DS of Figure 2.2 and (b)–(f) the clusters construction process. Each time a similarity edge is processed, it is highlighted in blue, the corresponding center nodes in green and the non-center ones in pink. The resulting equivalence clusters are shown in Figure 3.15.

Figure 3.15: The equivalence clusters (i.e., entities) derived from Center Clustering in Figure 3.14.

In a different line of work, *Maximum Clique Clustering* (MCC) [Draisbach et al., 2020] puts more emphasis on the structure of the similarity graph, rather than its edge weights. It iteratively removes the maximum clique along with its vertices until all nodes have been assigned to an equivalence cluster. It is remarkable that this approach applies even to unweighted similarity graphs, i.e., graphs where an edge connects two nodes/profiles that are likely matches, while the absence of an edge denotes unlikely matches.

MCC is generalized by *Extended Maximum Clique Clustering* [Draisbach et al., 2020], which removes maximal cliques from the similarity graph, but then enlarges them by adding edges that are incident to a minimum portion of their nodes.

This is similar to *GCluster* [Wang et al., 2016a], which enlarges the initial partitions by merging them as long as they create a δ-clique, i.e., a clique with v vertices, where every node is connected to at least $\delta \cdot (v - 1)$ others.

Finally, *SuperPart* [Reas et al., 2018] is a supervised approach that produces the final entities without requiring any manual parameter fine-tuning, while providing a confidence score for its output—unlike all unsupervised approaches. It operates in five consecutive steps: (i) it applies Connected Components with a threshold of 0.5, assuming that the edge weights correspond to matching probabilities; (ii) it converts every connected component into a complete graph; (iii) it applies a series of unsupervised clustering algorithms for Dirty ER to each complete graph, yielding a series of possible partitions; (iv) it defines a feature vector for each partition by considering a wide range of evidence—from the clustering algorithm that produced it to several graph metrics like its diameter or the minimum, maximum, average and median edge weight; and (v) it trains a binary classifier, preferably a Random Forest, and associates every possible partition with a score in [0, 1]. The partition with the maximum score is selected as the final result, with the score corresponding to the confidence.

Methods for Multi-source ER.   The Deduplication algorithms are still applicable [Saeedi et al., 2017, 2018a]. In the case of clean input DSs, *CLIP* [Saeedi et al., 2018b] achieves higher performance by distinguishing graph edges into three categories, depending on whether they correspond to the maximum weight per source for both adjacent nodes; special care is taken to ensure that every cluster contains at most one profile per input DS.

CHAPTER 4

Generation 2: Also Addressing Volume

The main difference between the 1st and the 2nd ER generation is the challenge of *Volume*, as the input DSs now comprise (dozens of) millions of profiles. The quality of input data remains the same, involving relatively homogeneous structured data. Therefore, the performance target is to combine accurate results with high scalability, tackling both Veracity and Volume. This is achieved through the same end-to-end workflow as in the 1st ER generation (see Figure 3.1). Internally, though, the steps rely on *parallelization*. Two types of parallelization are typically employed.

1. *Multi-core parallelization* distributes the processing among the available CPUs of a single system. This approach is also called *shared-memory parallelization*, as all CPUs have access to the same memory.

2. *Massive parallelization* distributes the processing among the available nodes of a cluster. This approach is also called *shared-nothing parallelization*, as every node and every process in each node have their independent memory.

The latter approach pertains mainly to the MapReduce framework [Dean and Ghemawat, 2008], which offers fault-tolerant, optimized execution for applications distributed across a set of independent nodes. In a nutshell, MapReduce splits the input data into smaller chunks that are then processed in parallel in two phases. First, a `map` function extracts intermediate (`key`, `value`) pairs from each partition of the input data. Then, a `reduce` function processes the list of values that correspond to the same intermediate key, regardless of the mapper that emitted them. These two functions form a MapReduce `job`. For complex algorithms, multiple jobs are typically required. In each job, a crucial aspect is the *load balancing algorithm* that distributes evenly the overall workload among the available nodes so as to avoid potential bottlenecks in the computation-intensive parts of the implementation.

Next, we discuss the main parallelization methods for each workflow step. The only exception is Schema Alignment, which lacks concrete methods based on multi-core or massive (i.e., MapReduce) parallelization. General parallelization approaches are discussed in Bellahsene et al. [2011].

4.1   BLOCKING

The local, non-learning blocking methods lend themselves naturally to MapReduce paralleliza-tion. The `map` function extracts from each profile one or more pairs of the form (`blocking_key`, `profile_id`). Each reducer then creates a block b_k for every distinct blocking key, aggregating all profiles that are associated with it. This approach lies at the core of the parallel implementa-tions provided by Dedoop [Kolb et al., 2012c] for various local, non-learning methods. Among the learning-based methods, only CBlock [Sarma et al., 2012] can be seamlessly adapted to MapReduce.

For global, non-learning blocking methods, the MapReduce parallelization requires mul-tiple, complex jobs in order to compute the similarities between the blocking keys. For example, Sorted Neighborhood is adapted to MapReduce in the following way [Kolb et al., 2012b]: the `map` function extracts the blocking key(s) from each profile, while a *partitioning* phase sorts all profiles in alphabetical order of their keys. The `reduce` function slides a window of fixed size within every partition. To compare the profiles close to the partition boundaries across different reducers, the `map` function replicates them, forwarding them to the respective reducers. A more complex approach consisting of three jobs is presented in Mestre et al. [2015] for parallelizing DCS and DCS++ according to the MapReduce framework.

Example 4.1   An example of the Sorted Neighborhood adaptation to MapReduce [Kolb et al., 2012b] is illustrated in Figure 4.1. SN is applied to the Dirty DS of Figure 2.2 using two mappers and two reducers and the same blocking keys and window size ($w = 4$) as in Example 3.3. A user-defined function assigns all profiles whose blocking key starts with a letter between "a" and "n" to Reducer 1 and the remaining profiles to Reducer 2. The `map` function generates the blocking key for every profile it receives as input and associates it with a composite key of the form [$b.p.key$], as shown in Figure 4.1; *key* stands for the blocking key of the profile, p for the *partition prefix*, which indicates the id of the reducer that should process the profile, and b for the *boundary prefix*, which is equal to p for original profiles and to $p + 1$ for the replicated ones—after sorting locally all input profiles according to the alphabetical order of their key, the `map` function identifies as replicated the profiles in the lowest $w − 1$ positions per partition prefix. During the partitioning phase, all profiles with $b = 1$ are sent to Reducer 1 and those with $b = 2$ to Reducer 2. Then, each reducer sorts alphabetically all input profiles. Reducer 2 ignores all replicated profiles apart from the $w − 1 = 3$ ones in the lowest positions of their partition (i.e., G10, G8, and G3), because the rest do not actually correspond to missed comparisons—they are compared in Reducer 1, as they were replicated redundantly, due to the local information of the mapper. Finally, every reducer slides a window of size $w = 4$ over the sorted profiles of each partition. The end result consists of the same blocks of comparisons, as in Example 3.3. Note that the profile replication functionality does not allow for missing the block $\{G10, G8, G3, G6\}$, despite the partitioning.

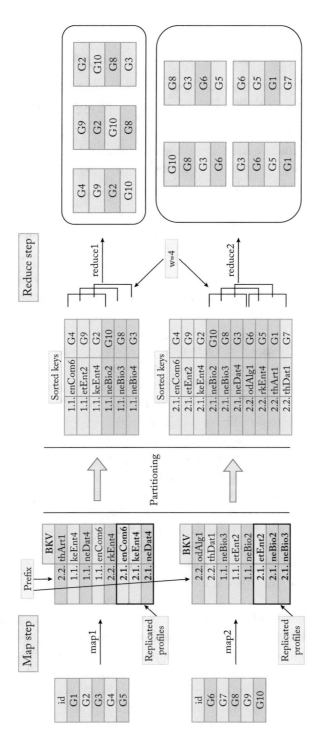

Figure 4.1: Sorted neighborhood adapted to MapReduce with profile replication.

4.2   MATCHING

We distinguish relevant techniques into the following two categories.

1. *Parallel pairwise ER methods* receive as input a set of blocks and distribute the verification of its candidate matches with MapReduce, based on the principle that every comparison is independent of the others.

2. *Parallel merge-based collective ER methods* use multicore or MapReduce parallelization to verify the candidate matches such that the newly discovered duplicates are efficiently distributed to all concurrent processes.

In both cases, special care is taken to distribute evenly the overall workload among the available resources so as to avoid potential bottlenecks. Below, we delve into the methods belonging to each category.

Load Balancing Methods.   To balance the computational cost of Matching on top of Blocking, these methods distribute evenly the pairwise comparisons of candidate matches among the available nodes in a MapReduce cluster.

BlockSplit [Kolb et al., 2012a] splits the bigger blocks into smaller sub-blocks and processes them in parallel. Special care is taken to ensure that every profile is compared not only to all profiles in its sub-block, but also to all profiles of its super-block, even if their sub-block is initially assigned to a different node. This yields additional network and I/O overhead, as profiles of split blocks are processed multiple times. Most importantly, BlockSplit may still lead to an unbalanced workload, due to sub-blocks of different size.

To overcome this issue, *PairRange* [Kolb et al., 2012a] splits evenly the comparisons in a set of blocks into a predefined number of partitions, by assigning every comparison to a particular partition id. To this end, it involves a single MapReduce job, whose mapper associates every profile p_i in block b_k with the output key $pid.k.i$, where pid denotes the index of the comparison range, i.e., the partition id. Then, the reducer groups together all profiles that have the same pid and block id, reproducing all comparisons of a particular partition.

Two more load balancing algorithms were presented in Yan et al. [2013]. Both rely on sketches in order to minimize memory consumption; the one aims to improve the space requirements of BlockSplit and the other of PairRange.

Dis-Dedup [Chu et al., 2016] goes beyond the above methods in that its cost model considers both the computational and the communication cost (e.g., network transfer time, local disk I/O time). The algorithm considers all possible cases of Blocking, from disjoint blocks stemming from a single blocking scheme to overlapping blocks derived from multiple blocking schemes. Most importantly, it provides strong theoretical guarantees that the overall maximum cost per reducer is within a small constant factor from the lower bounds.

Finally, several works examine the massive parallelization of string similarity join techniques in the context of the MapReduce framework. Prefix Filtering in combination with

Length, Positional, and Suffix filtering are parallelized in Vernica et al. [2010]. A similar approach that considers multiple prefix orders along with a load balancing technique is proposed in Rong et al. [2013], while inherently parallel methods are introduced in Deng et al. [2015] and Rong et al. [2017]. Their relative performance is experimentally assessed in Fier et al. [2018]. Vernica et al. [2010] performs best, but no technique scales well to very large datasets, due to the overhead of MapReduce and the high or skewed data replication between `map` and `reduce` tasks.

Methods for Parallel Merge-based Collective ER.   Early methods focus on multi-core parallelization.

The earliest one, *P-Swoosh* [Kawai et al., 2006], relies on the master-slave model. The master iteratively applies R-Swoosh [Benjelloun et al., 2009] to a subset of the input profiles, distributes the non-matching profiles to the slaves for further processing, and gathers, and synchronizes their partial results. Two types of load balancing are employed: (i) the horizontal one, which balances the workload among slave processors; and (ii) the vertical one, which balances the workload between the master and the slaves.

An approach based on the task graph model was proposed in Kim and Lee [2007], which examines the three different forms of ER with two input DSs: Clean-Clean ER, Dirty DS vs. Clean DS, and Dirty DS vs. Dirty DS (the last two cases are different forms of Dirty ER). The special characteristics of each ER task are levaraged in order to achieve high scalability and significantly improve the efficiency of P-Swoosh.

Another approach that uses the task graph model is *D-Swoosh* [Benjelloun et al., 2007], which parallelizes R-Swoosh [Benjelloun et al., 2009] using two types of functions: (i) the scope function, which assigns every profile to several CPUs; and (ii) the responsible function, which avoids redundant comparisons by choosing the CPU that will verify the profile pairs that cooccur in multiple CPUs. The more cores are available, the harder it is to define effective scope and especially responsible functions, a phenomenon that is investigated experimentally.

More recent approaches consider massive parallelization in MapReduce.

LSH is combined with R-Swoosh [Benjelloun et al., 2009] in Malhotra et al. [2014]: first, a MapReduce job is used for defining the blocks using LSH. Then, Apache Giraph[1] is used to iteratively execute the non-redundant comparisons in the blocks and to compute the transitivity closure of the detected profiles.

In Rastogi et al. [2011], a message-passing framework is proposed, based on MapReduce. During the `map` phase, multiple instances of the Matching algorithm run locally, inside every *active* block, while the `reduce` phase propagates the newly-identified matches to all blocks that might be influenced by them. Every block that contains any of the newly-matched profiles is marked as active, even if it has already been processed. This iterative algorithm terminates as soon as the list of active blocks becomes empty.

---

[1]http://giraph.apache.org

4.3   CLUSTERING

The methods of this optional step parallelize the Generation 1 techniques according to the MapReduce paradigm. The *FAst Multi-source Entity Resolution* (FAMER) framework [Saeedi et al., 2017, 2018a] introduces the distributed implementation of four established clustering algorithms on top of Apache Flink[2]: Connected Components, Center, Merge-Center, and Star Clustering. A parallel implementation of CLIP over Apache Flink is presented in Saeedi et al. [2018b], while Correlation Clustering is parallelized in Chierichetti et al. [2014] by picking many pivots (i.e., nodes from the similarity graph) in parallel and growing the clusters around them.

Example 4.2   Figure 4.2 illustrates the steps of applying the Parallel Center Clustering described in Saeedi et al. [2017]. The graph is the same as the one used in Example 3.7, divided into two partitions, which are labeled with light orange and blue colors in Figure 4.2a. In each round, one unassigned node is processed by each partition according to a predefined prioritization. In this example, it is assumed that nodes are always processed in ascending order of their ids.

For the node v to be processed, the edge $e = <v, u>$ with the highest weight must be found. If both v and u are unassigned and belong to the same partition, the node with the highest priority is labeled as center node and the other as non-center, as shown in Figure 4.2b for pairs $< G1, G7 >$ and $< G2, G5 >$.

If u is not a Center node and belongs to a different partition, then e is removed and the process is repeated for the edge with the highest weight among the remaining edges which are adjacent to v. Such an example occurs in Figure 4.2c, where Node $G3$ is processed for the blue partition and edge $< G3, G10 >$ is removed. In the next round, demonstrated in Figure 4.2d, $G3$ is assigned to $G8$'s cluster, which was previously labeled as Center node. In the same manner edge $< G5, G8 >$ is removed in 4.2d and the two nodes become singletons. The resulting equivalence clusters are illustrated in Figure 4.3 and coincide with those derived with the sequential algorithm in Example 3.7.

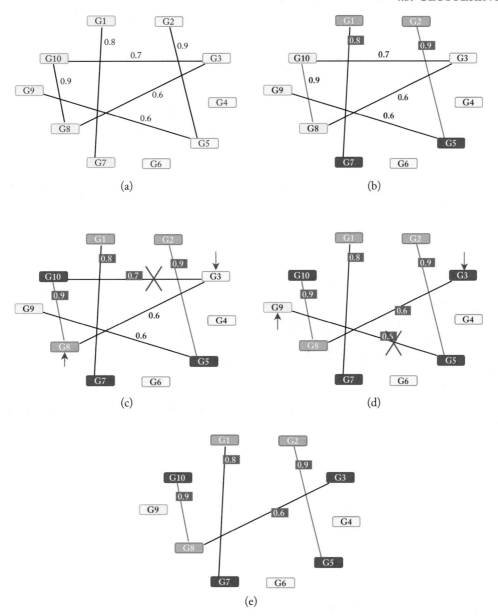

Figure 4.2: Applying Parallel Center Clustering to the graph in Figure 3.14: (a) is the similarity graph that is divided in two partitions: ($G1, G7, G8, G9, G10$) and ($G2, G3, G4, G5, G6$). (b)–(e) show the clusters construction process. Each time a similarity edge is processed, it is highlighted in blue, the corresponding center nodes in green and the non-center ones in pink. The resulting equivalence clusters are shown in Figure 4.3.

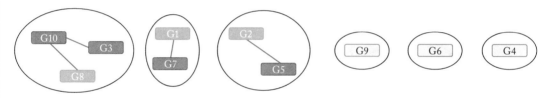

Figure 4.3: The equivalence clusters (i.e., entities) derived from Parallel Center Clustering in Figure 4.2.

CHAPTER 5

Generation 3: Also Addressing Variety

A shift in ER was marked by its 3rd generation, where the input comprises large volumes of semi-structured, unstructured, or highly heterogeneous structured data. This means that ER has to address not only Veracity and Volume, but also *Variety*, which is caused by the unprecedented levels of schema heterogeneity and noise as well as the loose schema binding of unclear semantics. For example, the Semantic Web includes almost 700 high-quality vocabularies with more than 35,000 properties and 28,000 classes.[1] In these settings, it is impossible to build and maintain a global schema through Schema Alignment [Golshan et al., 2017], thus rendering the schema-aware methods of the previous generations inapplicable.

For this reason, the end-to-end workflow of this generation, shown in Figure 5.1, consists of the following steps.

1. *Schema Refinement* differs from Schema Alignment in the previous generations in that it does not necessarily focus on identifying semantically identical attributes. Instead, it suffices to partition the attributes according to syntactic similarity so as to boost the performance of the next workflow steps [Hassanzadeh et al., 2013, Madhavan et al., 2007].

2. *Block Building* corresponds to Blocking in the previous generations, clustering together similar profiles into blocks so as to restrict the comparisons to profiles that are highly likely to be matching. Unlike Blocking, its functionality is schema-agnostic, i.e., decoupled from precise schema knowledge.

3. *Block Processing* further cuts down on the computational cost of ER by cleaning the original blocks from superfluous and redundant comparisons.

4. *Matching* verifies all matching candidates in the final set of blocks to create a similarity graph.

5. *Clustering* partitions the nodes of the similarity graph into entities.

Below, we investigate every step in more detail. Note that the sub-task of Clean-Clean ER (i.e., Definition 2.2) is also called **Co-reference Resolution** over unstructured data [Kejriwal and Miranker, 2015b, Soon et al., 2001] and **Link Discovery** over Semantic Web's Linked

---

[1] https://lov.linkeddata.es/dataset/lov/

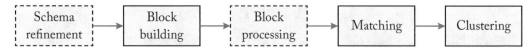

Figure 5.1: The 3rd generation of the end-to-end ER workflow. Dashed contours indicate optional steps.

Data [Nentwig et al., 2017b, Ngomo and Auer, 2011, Volz et al., 2009], where the goal is to identify missing `owl:sameAs` statements.

5.1 SCHEMA REFINEMENT

This optional step takes one of the following three forms.

(Large-scale) Ontology Alignment. There is a large body of works that aligns the concepts and the attributes between two, or more ontologies. A core methodology, called *instance-based ontology matching* [Otero-Cerdeira et al., 2015], relies on the similarity between the values related with every concept and attribute. Duan et al. [2012] focuses on processing a large number of profiles that include multiple types. It is based on locality-sensitive hashing techniques to first estimate the similarity between profiles and then the similarity of the profile types.

Another method, proposed in Dai et al. [2008], validates matches among multi-column schemas. It is based on statistical types structure from the data to detect the semantic types while also using the low integrability score to "invalidate" matches. The method from Kang and Naughton [2003] focused on column names that are "opaque" or very difficult to interpret. Processing first builds a dependency graph for the attributes in each data source by mining the instance values and then runs a graph matching algorithm to detect matches.

The *RiMOM* framework [Li et al., 2009] suggested an alternative methodology. The framework contains a collection of ontology alignment strategies. It automatically determines the methods to be used as well as the information to use in the similarity calculation, and also how to combine multiple methods. Two classes of ontology alignment strategies are used: (i) linguistic-based, such as edit-distance; and (ii) structured-based, focusing on detecting ontologies with similar graph structures.

Several established methods are also implemented in *AgreementMaker* [Cruz et al., 2009], an extensible tool with an intuitive graphical user interface. Its solutions operate on three layers: the first compares the concepts and the attributes between the two input ontologies, the second enriches the original results with structural or conceptual information and the third combines the results of multiple matchers from the previous two layers, producing the final set of schema mappings.

More details on the main techniques in the field can be found in books [Euzenat and Shvaiko, 2013] and surveys [Ochieng and Kyanda, 2018, Otero-Cerdeira et al., 2015, Shvaiko and Euzenat, 2013].

Schema Clustering.   This process receives the input DS(s) and returns as output clusters of *syntactically similar attributes*, i.e., attribute names that correspond to similar values and/or names, but not necessarily to the same meaning. Instead of producing clusters of semantically identical attributes (as does Schema Matching), its goal is to improve the performance of all subsequent steps in the end-to-end ER workflow [Madhavan et al., 2007]. For Block Building, this is accomplished by splitting large blocks into smaller ones, without separating pairs of duplicates, according to the schema clusters that are associated with every blocking key [Papadakis et al., 2013]. Block Processing uses the entropy inside every attribute cluster to refine the matching candidates in blocks, without actually executing them [Simonini et al., 2016]. This entropy can also be used for refining the profile similarities in Matching.

The *Attribute Clustering* algorithm [Papadakis et al., 2013] represents every attribute by the aggregation of all its values over the entire DS. All pairs of attribute representations are compared with each other and an *attribute graph* is formed, with every node corresponding to a distinct attribute. Then, an edge is added to connect each attribute to its most similar one. The transitive closure of the connected attributes forms disjoint clusters, with a *glue cluster* encompassing all nodes that are left alone. This process is generalized in Simonini et al. [2016] by allowing multiple edges per node in the attribute graph: every node is connected to all others with a similarity larger than α% of its maximum value similarity; for higher efficiency, LSH is used to estimate the Jaccard similarity between value aggregations.

The *SMaSh* framework [Hassanzadeh et al., 2013] operates in four steps. First, it loads a dataset that can be in variety of formats (XML, CSV, JSON, a relational database, or a SPARQL end-point). Second, it analyzes and indexes the values associated with every attribute, using a variety of techniques (e.g., token or q-gram analyzer). Third, it applies a novel search algorithm, *SMaSh-S* or *SMaSh-R*, that can be combined with any established similarity measure. Its goal is to find pairs of attributes from different DSs that exhibit a sufficiently high similarity in their values. Fourth, the detected attribute pairs are filtered through thresholds on heuristic measures like distinctiveness ("strenth") and coverage. The end result comprises a ranked list of syntactically similar pairs of attributes.

Schema Matching methods can also be used for this step as long as they scale to large schema spaces. Higher scalability and performance can be achieved by relaxing strong constraints for semantic equivalence, which is not a prerequisite in this case. For example, the LSH-based method in Duan et al. [2012] can be applied to Schema Clustering by adding all non-matched attribute names to a glue cluster.

Universal Schema.   A main issue in data integration is the schema mismatch between the source and target. Investigating how to eliminate this issue led to methods that combine the relations of all sources into a single one, which is referred to as a *universal schema*. Riedel et al. [2013] uses a universal schema for representing entities and relations (i.e., from textual patterns), while employing matrix factorization for learning implications among relations. An extension of this work focuses on allowing for deeper interactions between the sources by training tex-

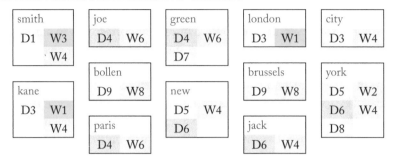

Figure 5.2: Applying token blocking to the DS of Figure 2.1 results in 10 blocks, in total.

tual relations and knowledge base jointly [Toutanova et al., 2015]. A follow-up study further enhances this technique by adopting probabilistic models of matrix factorization and collaborative filtering, in order to incorporate correlations between relations and textual patterns through pairs [Verga and McCallum, 2016]. Its main advantage is the ability to make predictions about pairs appearing in new textual patterns.

5.2   BLOCK BUILDING

Unlike the previous blocking methods, these approaches require no schema knowledge. Instead, they exclusively rely on the content, name or identity of profiles in order to decide whether they are potentially matches. In this way, they are able to effectively resolve heterogeneous and loosely structured data across domains, such as those stemming from the (Semantic) Web [Papadakis et al., 2011b, 2012, 2013].

The cornerstone schema-agnostic method for semi-structured data is *Token Blocking* [Papadakis et al., 2011b]. At its core, lies the assumption that duplicates should share at least a common token in their attribute values. Therefore, it uses as blocking keys the set of all tokens in all attribute values of a profile. Each distinct token t defines a new block b_t, essentially building an inverted index of profiles. Two profiles are placed in the same block, if they share a token in their values, regardless of the associated attributes.

Example 5.1   Figure 5.2 shows the 12 blocks generated by applying Token Blocking to the profiles of Figure 2.1. All attribute values are tokenized on special characters and then lowercased. Tokens like "serge" and "canada" create no blocks, as they appear in just one profile (recall that each block contains at least two profiles). Token Blocking successfully places all duplicate pairs in at least one common block, but yields an extremely high computational cost: it involves 21 candidate matches, which is much lower than the 80 profile pairs considered by the brute-force approach, but much higher than the 6 profile pairs that are actually duplicates.

The crude operation of Token Blocking can be improved by reducing the large number of its superfluous and redundant comparisons without affecting those involving duplicates. This way, precision (i.e., *PQ*) increases without any (significant) impact on recall (i.e., *PC*). Four methods have been proposed toward this end.

The first one is *Attribute Clustering Blocking* [Papadakis et al., 2013]. As described above, it requires the common tokens of two profiles to appear in *syntactically similar attributes*, i.e., in attributes that contain similar values but are not necessarily semantically matching (unlike Schema Alignment).

Example 5.2   To illustrate the functionality of Attribute Clustering, consider again the profiles of Figure 2.1. Using a character-based similarity measure, such as edit distance, we get the attribute graph in Figure 5.3a, which depicts the transitive closure of the pairs of most similar attributes between D_1 and D_2. These attributes are then clustered in the partitions of Figure 5.3b. The sets of blocks constructed for each cluster is shown in Figure 5.3c. We observe that the block $b^{york} = \{D5, D6, D8, W2, W4\}$ of Token Blocking is now split into two different blocks, since the key "york" appears in both attribute clusters, as shown in Figure 5.3c. Thus, the six candidate matches of the original block have been reduced to just $(1 + 2 =)3$, while the duplicates $< D8, W2 >$ and $< D4, W6 >$ remain in the same block (b^{york}_{AC1} and b^{york}_{AC2}, respectively). Nevertheless, the new set of blocks still contains redundant comparisons (e.g., $D6$ and $W4$ still share three blocks) as well as superfluous ones.

A different approach is followed by *Prefix-Infix(-Suffix) Blocking* [Papadakis et al., 2012], which exploits the naming pattern in the profiles' URIs. The *prefix* describes the domain of the URI, the *infix* is a local identifier, and the optional *suffix* contains details about the format, or a named anchor [Papadakis et al., 2010]. For example, consider the URI `http://liris.cnrs.fr/olivier.aubert/foaf.rdf#me`; the prefix is `http://liris.cnrs.fr`, the infix is `olivier.aubert` and the suffix is `foaf.rdf#me`. In this context, this method uses as blocking keys the (URI) infixes along with the tokens in the profiles of literal values. Yet, its applicability is constrained by the extent to which common naming policies are followed within a KB. In a favorable scenario, the infixes allow for detecting duplicates, even if their literal values share no tokens.

The third approach to improving Token Blocking is *TYPiMatch* [Ma and Tran, 2013]. It classifies the profiles of heterogeneous DSs into different, possibly overlapping type; e.g., products in a Web repository can be distinguished into computers, cameras, etc. TYPiMatch applies Token Blocking independently to the profiles of each type. It creates a co-occurrence graph, where every node corresponds to a token in any attribute value and every edge connects two tokens if both conditional probabilities of co-occurrence exceed a predetermined threshold. The maximal cliques from the co-occurrence graph are then extracted and merged if their overlap

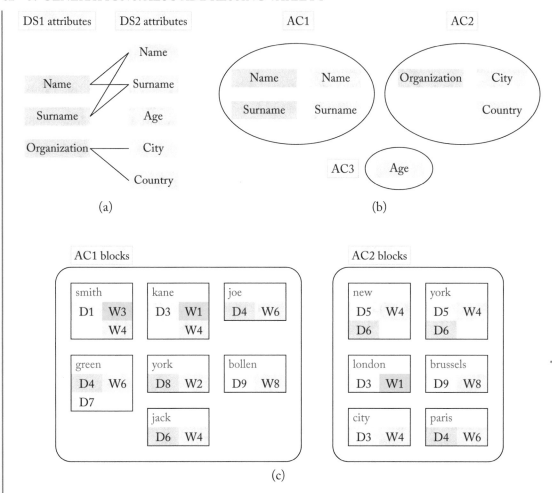

Figure 5.3: The steps of Attribute Clustering Blocking: (a) the attribute graph capturing the pairs of most similar attributes; (b) the connected attributes of the graph forming the disjoint attribute clusters; and (c) a block is created for every token in the attribute values of each cluster.

exceeds another threshold. The resulting clusters correspond to the types, with every profile participating in all types to which its tokens belong.

Finally, *RDFKeyLearner* [Song and Heflin, 2011] applies Token Blocking independently to the values of specific attributes, which are selected through the following process: each attribute is associated with a *discriminability* score, which amounts to the portion of distinct values over all its values in the given DS. If this is lower than a predetermined threshold, the attribute is ignored due to limited diversity, i.e., too many profiles have the same value(s). For each attribute

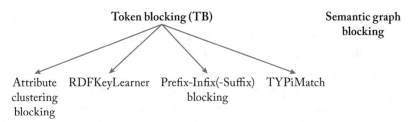

Figure 5.4: The genealogy tree of the non-learning block building methods, based on Papadakis et al. [2020b].

with high discriminability, its *coverage* is estimated, i.e., the portion of profiles that contain it. The harmonic mean of discriminability and coverage is then computed for all valid attributes and the one with the maximum score is selected for defining blocking keys as long as its score exceeds another predetermined threshold. If not, the selected attribute is combined with all other attributes and the process is repeated.

On another line of research, *Semantic Graph Blocking* [Nin et al., 2007] is based exclusively on the relations between profiles using, for example, foreign keys in a database or links in RDF data. It completely disregards attribute values, building a collaborative graph, where every node corresponds to a profile and every edge connects two associated profiles. For instance, the collaborative graph for a bibliographic data collection can be formed by mapping every author to a node and adding edges between co-authors. Then a new block b_i is formed for each node n_i, containing all nodes connected with n_i through a path. The only requirement is that the path length or the block size do not exceed specific limits.

Learning-based Methods.   *Hetero* [Kejriwal and Miranker, 2014] converts the input DSs into heterogeneous structured datasets using property tables. Then, it maps every profile to a normalized TF vector and applies an adapted Hungarian algorithm with linear scalability to produce positive and negative feature vectors. Finally, it applies *FisherDisjunctive* [Kejriwal and Miranker, 2013] with bagging for robust performance. Similarly, *Extended DNF BSL* [Kejriwal and Miranker, 2015a] combines an established instance-based schema matcher with weighted set covering to learn DNF blocking schemes with at most k attributes.

Discussion.   The relation of the aforementioned methods is depicted in Figure 5.4. Token Blocking is the root method, as it relies on the simplest assumption in order to maximize recall: it merely requires that duplicates share at least one common token in their values. Extensive experiments have demonstrated that this assumption holds for KBs in the *center of the LOD cloud* [Christophides et al., 2015, Efthymiou et al., 2015b]. Yet, this coarse-grained approach typically leads to very low precision, since most of the pairs sharing a common word are non-matches.

TYPiMatch attempts to raise precision, by categorizing the given profiles into overlapping types, but its recall typically drops to a large extent, due to the noisy, schema-agnostic detection of entity types; it is also time-consuming and rather sensitive to its parameter configuration [Papadakis et al., 2016b].

More significant are the improvements introduced by Attribute Clustering Blocking and Prefix-Infix(-Suffix) Blocking. The former, which is more general and effective, increases precision by further requiring that the common tokens of matches appear in syntactically (not semantically) similar attributes. The latter applies only to RDF data, disregarding most tokens from the URIs of attribute values, considering only their most distinguishing part, i.e., their infix. However, extensive experiments have shown that even these advanced schema-agnostic blocking methods perform poorly when applied to KBs from the *periphery of the LOD cloud* [Christophides et al., 2015, Efthymiou et al., 2015b]. The reason is that they exclusively consider the noisy content of profiles, disregarding the valuable evidence that is provided by contextual information, such as the neighboring profiles, which might be of different types, but are connected via important relations.

Comparing these methods with those of the previous generations, we can deduce that they follow a different philosophy. Blocking in Generations 1 and 2 aims to maximize recall and precision at once, in a single procedure, whereas Generation 3 involves two steps [Papadakis and Nejdl, 2011]: the creation of blocks, i.e., Block Building, which is discussed in this section and aims to maximize recall, and Block Processing, which is discussed in the next section and aims to raise the originally low precision by orders of magnitude. This two-step approach has two advantages: (i) it applies to data of any structuredness, from relational data to free-text profiles; and (ii) it simplifies parameter configuration, involving neither complex combinations of (parts of) attribute values nor labeled instances. Rather than human intervention or expert knowledge, the robustness of Block Building emanates from the high levels of *redundancy* it employs, placing every profile in a multitude of blocks.

Note, though, that the non-learning Blocking methods of Generation 1 are *compatible* with the schema-agnostic functionality of Block Building. They can be easily adapted to it by treating every distinct attribute value token as a primary blocking key, to which they apply their transformation (e.g., sorting, suffix or q-grams extraction) [Papadakis et al., 2015]. This adaptation enables traditional schema-aware methods to consistently score very high recall ($\gg$85%), while simplifying their configuration to the extent of waiving the requirement for domain knowledge [Papadakis et al., 2015]. Most importantly, this adaptation enables them to address not only Volume, but also Variety. The resulting precision, though, is extremely low [Papadakis et al., 2015], thus necessitating Block Processing, which is discussed next.

5.3   BLOCK PROCESSING

The core characteristic of block building methods is that their blocks achieve very high recall at the cost of a large number of *redundant* and *superfluous comparisons*, which appear in multiple blocks and involve non-matching profiles, respectively. The goal of Block Processing is to discard both types of comparisons in order to enhance the precision of schema-agnostic blocks at a limited cost in recall. Depending on the granularity of their functionality, we distinguish the relevant techniques into the following.

1. The *block-centric methods*, which rely on the coarse-grained characteristics of blocks. Such techniques are efficient, but lack in accuracy, as their crude processing cannot control its impact on recall (in terms of matching comparisons).

2. The *profile-centric methods*, which involve a more fine-grained operation that considers individual profiles, assessing the importance of each block independently for each profile it contains.

3. The *comparison-centric methods*, which operate at the level of profile pairs in order to decide whether they should be compared or not (in case of redundant or superfluous comparisons). Their fine-grained processing is more accurate than the other categories, at the price of a higher computational cost.

Below, we examine each category separately.

Block-centric Methods.   *Block Purging* a-priori discards blocks with a size [Papadakis et al., 2011b] or *cardinality* (i.e., number of pairwise comparisons) [Papadakis et al., 2013] higher than a limit.

Block Pruning [Papadakis et al., 2011b] orders blocks from the smallest to the largest one, terminating their processing as soon as the cost of identifying new matches exceeds a threshold. Both methods are equivalent to discarding stop-words, i.e., very frequent words that convey little information about a profile, such as "the" or "to." Such words add significant computational cost, without contributing useful similarity evidence or unique candidate matches, which share no other block.

A similar approach is the dynamic blocking algorithm in [McNeill et al., 2012], which splits large blocks into sub-blocks, "until they are all of tractable size."

The same idea lies at the core of *Size-based Block Clustering* [Fisher et al., 2015], a hierarchical clustering approach that transforms a set of blocks into a new one where all block sizes lie within a specified size range. In essence, it merges recursively small blocks that correspond to similar blocking keys, while splitting large blocks into smaller ones. At its core, lies a penalty function that controls the trade-off between block quality and block size.

Entity-centric Methods.   For the moment, this category includes only *Block Filtering* [Papadakis et al., 2016a], which removes every profile from the least important of its blocks. The main assumption is that the larger a block is, the less important it is for its profiles. Thus, it orders the input blocks in ascending order of cardinality and retains every profile p_i in the N_i smallest blocks, where $N_i = \lfloor r \times |B_i| \rfloor$ and $r \in [0, 1]$ is the ratio of Block Filtering. Setting $r = 0.8$ was verified to significantly raise efficiency, pruning $\geq 50\%$ of the overall comparisons, while having a negligible impact on recall [Papadakis et al., 2016a].

Comparison-centric Methods.   The earliest method of this type is *Iterative Blocking* [Whang et al., 2009b]. Its functionality depends on the outcomes of the Matching method: whenever a new pair of duplicates is detected, their profiles are merged and replaced by the unified profile in all blocks that contain them. This way, all redundant comparisons of the matched profiles are discarded. The already examined blocks that contain either of the matched profiles are reprocessed in an effort to exploit the new information in the merged profile for identifying more duplicates.

Another iterative approach depending on the matching results is *HARRA* [Kim and Lee, 2010], which relies on an LSH-based procedure to dynamically hash similar profiles into the same buckets (i.e., blocks). Inside every bucket, all pairwise comparisons are executed and pairs of matches are merged into new profiles. The new profiles are hashed into the existing hash tables so as to optimize memory usage. This procedure runs until convergence (i.e., no entities are merged) or until another, stricter stopping criterion is satisfied (e.g., the portion of merged profiles drops below a predetermined threshold). In every iteration, special care is taken to avoid redundant and superfluous comparisons.

Another matching-aware approach to discard redundant and superfluous comparisons is presented in Gazzarri and Herschel [2020], based on (scalable) Bloom filters to minimize the space requirements. It iterates over all pairwise comparisons in a set of blocks and lookups every one of them in the Bloom filter. A comparison that is already included in it is skipped, otherwise it is executed and its id is inserted in the data structure. This is an approximate algorithm, as false positives are possible, i.e., the lookup returns `true` for comparisons that are actually absent from the Bloom filter. The rate of false positives actually increases as more comparisons are inserted in the data structure. To minimize them, the blocks are sorted in increasing size.

All other methods of this type are independent of Matching. The simplest one, *Comparison Propagation* [Papadakis et al., 2011c], discards all redundant comparisons from any set of blocks without any impact on recall. After comparing two profiles in a block, this comparison is not repeated in any other block they share.

More advanced techniques belong to the family of *Meta-blocking* methods [Papadakis et al., 2014a]; they discard all redundant comparisons from any set of blocks, but go beyond Comparison Propagation, as they also target the majority of superfluous comparisons. Their scope, though, is restricted to *redundancy-positive* sets of blocks, where the more blocks two profiles share, the more likely they are to be matching. Their functionality consists of two logical steps.

1. The original set of blocks B is transformed into the *blocking graph* G_B, where the nodes correspond to the profiles of B, and the edges connect the candidate matches. There is at most one edge for every pair of profiles, regardless of its co-occurrence frequency in blocks, thus eliminating all redundant comparisons.

2. Every edge is associated with a weight that is proportional to the likelihood that the adjacent candidate matches are matching. This weight quantifies the evidence that is given by the degree of overlap between the block lists associated with the two profiles. Low-weighted edges are less likely to correspond to a match, so they are pruned. The pruned blocking graph G'_B is transformed into a new set of blocks B' by creating a new block for every retained edge.

Various schemes have been proposed for edge weighting [Papadakis et al., 2014a, Simonini et al., 2016]. They exclusively consider schema-agnostic information from the given blocks, such as the number of common blocks, their size etc. Based on edge weighting, the *pruning scheme* decides which edges (i.e., candidate matches) will be retained. The main pruning schemes are the following.

- *Weighted Edge Pruning* (*WEP*) retains all edges with a weight higher than the overall mean one.

- *Cardinality Edge Pruning* (*CEP*) retains the top-K edges of the entire blocking graph.

- *Weighted Node Pruning* (*WNP*) retains for every node the incident edges that exceed the average edge weight in the entire neighborhood.

- *Cardinality Node Pruning* (*CNP*) retains the top-k edges in each node neighborhood.

Several variations of these algorithms have been proposed: CEP is altered in Zhang et al. [2017a] such that it retains the top-weighted edges whose cumulative weight is higher than a specific portion of the total sum of edge weights; *Reciprocal WNP* and *CNP* [Papadakis et al., 2016a] retain an edge in the blocking graph if it satisfies the pruning criteria in both adjacent nodes' neighborhoods; *BLAST* [Simonini et al., 2016] combines WNP with a weight threshold per edge, which depends on the maximum weights in the adjacent nodes' neighborhoods.

Example 5.3   The functionality of Meta-blocking is illustrated in Figure 5.5. The input set of blocks in Figure 5.5a—produced by some redundancy-positive blocking method—contains five distinct profiles. Figure 5.5b depicts the respective blocking graph, with one node for each profile and one edge for each pair of candidate matches. Note that there are five edges, whereas the input blocks involve eight comparisons: the simple blocking graph discards all redundant comparisons, without considering the edge weights. The edge weights, which in this case indicate the number of common blocks per candidate match, aim exclusively to detect the superfluous comparisons. In Figure 5.5c, the superfluous comparisons are discarded using the WEP pruning algorithm: every edge with a weight lower than the average one ($8/5 = 1.4$) is removed. A new block is then created for each retained edge, as shown in Figure 5.5d.

Note that *Canopy Clustering* [McCallum et al., 2000] can be considered as a Meta-blocking method, too, even though it was originally proposed for clustering and was adapted

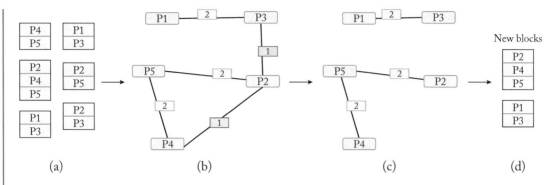

(a)   (b)   (c)   (d)

Figure 5.5: Applying Meta-blocking: (a) the input set of redundancy-positive blocks, (b) the corresponding blocking graph, whose edges are weighted according to the number of blocks shared by the adjacent profiles, (c) the pruned blocking graph after applying WEP, and (d) the new set of blocks.

as a 1st-generation blocking method in Christen [2012b]. This adaptation used the keys of Q-grams Blocking for deriving a cheap similarity measure, but there is no restriction for applying it exclusively on top of Q-grams Blocking. We could generalize its cheap similarity to exploit the blocking keys of any redundancy-positive blocking method, turning it into a Meta-blocking technique [Papadakis et al., 2018]. Similarly, *Extended Canopy Clustering* [Christen, 2012b] can be considered as a Meta-blocking technique, too.

In all cases, the main restriction of Meta-blocking is that its blocking graph supports a single type of blocks. Yet, composite blocking schemes may also be constructed on different types of blocks, as explained above. To accommodate them, Meta-blocking has been extended with a *Disjunctive Blocking Graph* [Efthymiou et al., 2019], which has the same set of vertices as the simple blocking graph, but associates every edge with a feature vector. Every dimension in this vector corresponds to a weight from a different set of blocks.

Another family of Meta-blocking algorithms that focuses on the edge weights between the profiles in each block is presented in Nascimento et al. [2019]. *Low Entity Co-occurrence Pruning* (LECP) cleans every block from a specific portion of the profiles with the lowest average edge weights. *Large Block Size Pruning* (LBSP) applies LECP only to the blocks whose size exceeds the average block size. *Low Block Co-occurrence Pruning* (LBCP) removes every profile from the blocks, where it is connected with the lowest average weights with the rest of the profiles. *CooSlicer* enforces a maximum block size constraint, $|b|_{max}$, to all input blocks. In blocks larger than $|b|_{max}$, all profiles are sorted in decreasing order of average edge weight, and the $|b|_{max}$ top-ranked profiles are iteratively placed into a new block. *Low Block Co-occurrence Excluder* (LBCE) discards a specific portion of the blocks with the lowest average edge weight among their profiles.

On another line of research, *SPAN* [Shu et al., 2011] converts a set of blocks into a matrix M, where the rows correspond to profiles and the columns to the TF-IDF similarity of their blocking keys (tokens or q-grams). Then, the profile-profile matrix is defined as $A = MM^T$. A spectral clustering algorithm converts A into a binary tree, where the root node contains all profiles and every leaf node is a disjoint subset of profiles. The Newman–Girvan modularity is used as the stopping criterion for the bipartition of the tree. Blocks are then derived from a search procedure that carries out comparisons inside the leaf nodes and across the neighboring ones.

Finally, *Transitive LSH* [Steorts et al., 2014] converts the blocks extracted from LSH into an unweighted blocking graph and applies a community detection algorithm (e.g., Clauset et al. [2004]) to partition the graph nodes into disjoint clusters, which will become the new blocks. The process, which can be generalized to apply on top of any blocking method, finishes when the size of the largest cluster is lower than a predetermined threshold.

Learning-based Methods.   *Supervised Meta-blocking* [Papadakis et al., 2014b] formalizes WEP, CNP, and CEP as binary classification tasks, associating every edge with a vector that comprises a set of representative features. Every feature vector is then given as input to a classifier, which labels it as "`likely match`" or "`unlikely match;`" edges with the former label correspond to retained candidate matches, while the other edges are discarded from the blocking graph. In this way, the simple, non-learning pruning rules of the form "*if weight < threshold then discard edge*" are replaced by composite pruning models that have been learned from labeled data. To restrict the computational cost, a minimal set of comprehensive features is used.

To minimize the labeling effort of Supervised Meta-blocking, *BLOSS* [Bianco et al., 2018] carefully selects a training set that is up to 40 times smaller, but retains the original performance. Using a particular weighting scheme, it partitions the unlabeled instances into similarity levels and applies rule-based active sampling inside every level. Then, it cleans the sample from non-matching outliers with high Jaccard similarity of associated block lists.

Discussion.   We observe that most methods involve a comparison-centric functionality that applies only to redundancy-positive blocks. Their relation is depicted in Figure 5.6. Note that they are incompatible with each other: at most one of them can be applied to a given set of blocks, because the restructured blocks they produce are deprived of any redundancy that is necessary for further pruning. Thus, BLAST [Simonini et al., 2016] or Disjunctive Blocking Graph [Efthymiou et al., 2019] should be preferred, as they achieve the top performance among comparison-centric methods. However, a comparative analysis is required in order to evaluate the relative performance of these two methods. In any case, there is plenty of room for improving the accuracy of comparison-centric methods, as their precision remains rather low [Efthymiou et al., 2019, Papadakis et al., 2016b, Simonini et al., 2016].

The remaining block- and profile-centric methods are complementary with each other, as they target different aspects of a set of blocks. Hence, it makes no sense to seek the top performer

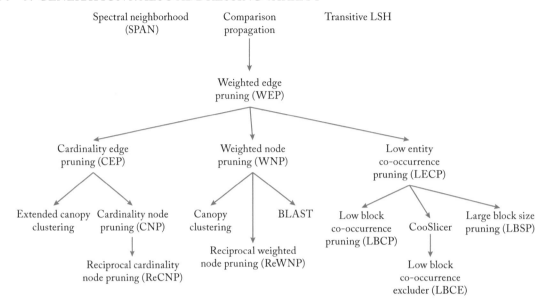

Figure 5.6: The genealogy tree of the non-learning, comparison-centric Block Processing methods, based on Papadakis et al. [2020b].

among them. Instead, every end-to-end ER workflow should involve as many of these methods as possible—they are indispensable for reducing the search space of the selected comparison-centric approach to a significant extent [Papadakis et al., 2016b].

Note that only three methods depend on Matching: Block Pruning, Iterative Blocking, and HARRA. They assume a perfect matcher, but exploit it in different ways. The first one employs the rate of detected duplicates as a signal for prematurely terminating the entire procedure, whereas the other two use the matched profiles as a means of detecting more matches. A more realistic scenario should involve a noisy matcher, investigating its errors' effect on the overall performance. Note that the approach in Gazzarri and Herschel [2020] does not depend on the outcome of Matching. It merely performs Matching during the cleaning of comparisons so as to reduce the false positives and, thus, its impact on recall.

5.4   MATCHING

Similar to the homonymous step in previous generations, Matching receives as input a set of blocks and produces as output a similarity graph. We distinguish the relevant techniques into two categories.

1. The **context-based** approaches counterbalance the high levels of schema noise conveyed by Variety through the neighbor similarity, which is determined by the relations between

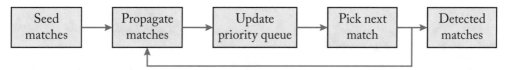

Figure 5.7: The iterative, collective algorithm used in context-based matching.

profiles. Such methods typically involve an iterative processing that discovers duplicate profiles gradually and propagates the latest matches to related profiles that could benefit from them [Lacoste-Julien et al., 2013, Li et al., 2009, Suchanek et al., 2011].

2. The **context-free** approaches rely exclusively on the information in an individual pair of profiles. They tackle Variety through a fully schema-agnostic approach, or assume that the main part of the input schema(ta) has been cleaned or aligned through large-scale ontology matching techniques, which can process thousands of different attributes/predicates [Ochieng and Kyanda, 2018].

We elaborate on the two categories in the following.

5.4.1   CONTEXT-BASED MATCHING

Most methods of this type are non-learning and crafted for Clean-Clean ER, exploiting the 1-1 correspondence between the input DSs. With minor modifications, they implement the algorithm depicted in Figure 5.7: they are bootstrapped with a small set of reliable seed matches. Using a complex similarity measure that combines attribute value similarity with neighbor similarity, they propagate the initial matches to their neighbors. They place all candidate matches in a priority queue, sorted in descending overall similarity, as it is derived from the evidence that is available so far. In every iteration, the top pair is considered a match as long as it satisfies a constraint. In such cases, the similarity of the neighbors is recomputed and their position in the priority queue is updated accordingly.

In more detail, *SiGMa* [Lacoste-Julien et al., 2013] defines as seed matches the profiles with *identical names*, i.e., identical values for the attribute with the highest distinctiveness. This assumes that part of the schema has been refined and aligned. It also requires that the top pair is popped from the priority queue only if it exceeds a predetermined threshold.

LINDA [Böhm et al., 2012] alings the schemata of the input DSs based on the edit distance between their attribute names and terminates after a specific number of iterations, or after the priority queue becomes empty.

RiMOM-IM [Li et al., 2009, Shao et al., 2016] defines as seed matches the profiles co-occurring in blocks of size 2. Similar to SiGMa, it assumes the partial alignment of the input schemata, possibly through human intervention. It also coins the *"one-left object"* heuristic: if two duplicates p_1 and p'_1 are connected via aligned relations r and r' and all their neighbors via r and r', except p_2 and p'_2, have been matched, too, then p_2 and p'_2 are also considered matches.

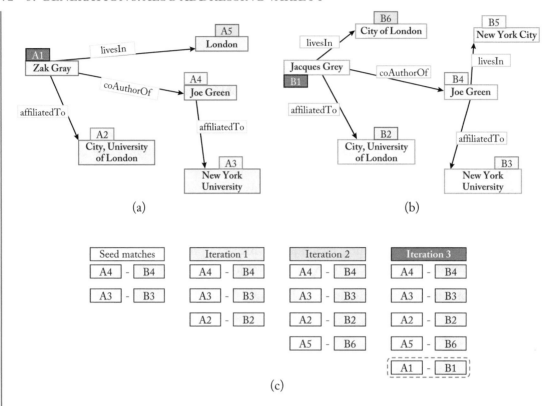

Figure 5.8: Applying SiGMa: (a) DS A, (b) DS B, and (c) the progress of the matches propagation process.

PARIS [Suchanek et al., 2011] considers as seed matches the profiles having identical values for all attributes. Based on them, it partially aligns the given schemata. This information is exploited by a probabilistic model that relies on the *functionality* of each attribute, i.e., the extent to which its values can be used as keys that uniquely identify a profile (e.g., the email address is a fully functional property).

Example 5.4   Figure 5.8 shows an example of SiGMa's functionality on the Knowledge Bases A and B, which appear in Figures 5.8a and b, respectively. Figure 5.8c illustrates a possible evolution of the matches' propagation process. The initial (seed) matches include only the profiles with identical names (i.e., $A3 - B3$ and $A4 - B4$). In each iteration, both string and graph similarity measures are considered to evaluate candidate pairs. The new pairs being matched at each iteration are labeled with the same color as the corresponding iteration in Figure 5.8c. In iteration 3, profiles A1 and B1 share three pairs of neighbors which have already been matched together. Their high graph similarity indicates them as duplicates, even though their string similarity is equal to 0, since their names have no common tokens.

Other iterative works rely on random walks. *HolisticEM* [Pershina et al., 2015] builds a graph, whose nodes correspond to candidate matches, i.e., profile pairs that share at least one attribute value token. The graph is then expanded by adding edges between related pairs, taking special care to remove conflicting edges and nodes. The initial edge weights, estimated with cosine similarity on IDF weights, are iteratively propagated to neighboring nodes with Personalized PageRank until convergence.

BIGMAT [Assi et al., 2019] builds a graph, where the nodes correspond to profiles, the edges connect pairs with at least one common attribute value token, and their weights are proportionate to attribute value and neighbor similarity. An affinity-preserving random walk is applied on the graph to estimate the matching likelihood of every profile pair. Edges with very low final weights are discarded as non-matches. For higher efficiency, pairs with identical unique *labels* are directly considered as matches—the predicates that act as labels are automatically determined as the attributes with very high discriminativeness and coverage.

MinoanER [Efthymiou et al., 2016, 2018, 2019] goes beyond these works by turning context-based Matching into a non-iterative process that involves just four consecutive steps, with each one applying a matching rule:

1. it leverages data statistics to match profiles with similar names,

2. it detects duplicates with high attribute value similarity,

3. it detects nearly similar matches using a combination of value and neighbor similarity, and

4. it uses reciprocal evidence for refining the detected duplicates.

For high efficiency, all similarities are extracted from sets of blocks, rather than complex string comparisons.

5.4.2   CONTEXT-FREE MATCHING

The methods of this category are distinguished into supervised, unsupervised, and collective, similar to the Matching methods of Generation 1.

Supervised Methods.   A popular approach is to learn matching rules, which are also called *link specification* or *linkage rules*, through genetic programming.

GenLink [Isele and Bizer, 2012] represents complex rules through an operator tree that combines various similarity measures and thresholds nonlinearly (through aggregation operators). This representation also encompasses transformation operators, which allow for normalizing the attribute values to be compared, despite the high levels of noise and schema heterogeneity in the input DSs. A random population of rules is initially produced and is iteratively evolved through the common operators (mutation, crossover, and reproduction) until maximizing the F-Measure over the labeled instances.

A similar approach is *EAGLE* [Ngomo and Lyko, 2012]. It minimizes the number of required labeled instances through active learning, using a query-by-committee scheme to infer the most informative instances from the classifier's disagreement.

COALA [Ngomo et al., 2013] further reduces the required number of pairs to be labeled by considering their inter-correlation in two ways. The first one partitions the unlabeled pairs into disjoint clusters according to the similarity of their feature vectors so that it suffices to select a single, representative instance per cluster. The second approach employs a complex activation-spreading mechanism that infers the informativeness of every unlabeled pair from its correlation with all other instances, not only the most similar ones that probably belong to the same class.

Unlike the above methods which assume DSs with aligned ontologies, a schema-agnostic supervised is proposed in Giang [2015]. It defines a set of features that are independent of schema information, considering exclusively the label of each instance (i.e., its name), the textual description of its attributes as well as the text, dates, numbers and links (URIs) in the attribute values. Specific comparison functions are applied to each type of feature, yielding a 12-dimensional vector for every profile pair. A binary classifier is then learned through AdaBoost in combination with Random Forests. In case of insufficient labeled instances for the input DSs, a classical transfer learning algorithm, namely TrAdaBoost, is used instead.

A more advanced, graph-based approach is implemented by *Certus* [Kwashie et al., 2019]. It generalizes matching rules into graph patterns, called *graph differential dependencies* (GDDs), and proposes an algorithm for learning them automatically. The algorithm starts with detecting atomic GDDs and continues with their conjunctions, building a hierarchy of non-redundant GDDs. To apply the learned GDDs efficiency, Certus prunes the search space of candidate matches through Token Blocking, Weighted Edge Pruning, and a minimum threshold on the aggregate profile similarity.

Unsupervised Methods. Similar to Generation 1, unsupervised methods aim to learn matching rules effectively, while waiving the need for a large labeled dataset.

CHALD [Rivero and Ruiz, 2020] relies entirely on the statistics that can be efficiently derived from the input DS(s) without any labeling. First, it selects the most reliable attribute names for matching rules through the harmonic mean of universality and uniqueness. The former quantifies the coverage of an attribute name, i.e., the portion of profiles that contain it, while the latter estimates its distinctiveness, i.e., the portion of its unique attribute values. High values for both measures indicate an attribute that can act as a primary key. Then, the best matching rules are defined as those with a high singularity score (i.e., entropy), which indicates that few profile pairs are matching, while their vast majority are non-matching.

More advanced approaches rely on self-learning. *ObjectCoref* [Hu et al., 2011] receives a single URI as input and builds a kernel with duplicate profiles that are identified through five

OWL predicates, such as `owl:sameAs`. These positive instances are used for iteratively learning the most discriminative attribute-value pairs, which can effectively detect additional duplicates in the unlabeled pairs. For higher accuracy, an association rule mining algorithm is tailored to discovering the most discriminative co-occurring pairs of attribute-value pairs (e.g., latitude and longitude).

In Kejriwal and Miranker [2015b], a weakly labeled dataset is automatically generated by considering as positive instances the profiles pairs with a similarity score higher than a strict threshold. Using these "matches," the attribute names with high overlap in their values are aligned—without requiring that they are semantically equivalent. The values of the aligned attributes are compared with string similarity measures to convert the profile pairs into feature vectors. An SVM with a Radial Basis Function is then trained over the resulting vectors.

An approach based on genetic programming is presented in Nikolov et al. [2012]. The matching rules are represented as weighted, linear functions of similarity measures that compare the values of specific attribute pairs. Their results are filtered through a threshold on the aggregate similarity or through the nearest neighbor criterion, in the case of Clean-Clean ER. The common genetic operators are iteratively applied to an initially random population of rules until convergence. Due to the lack of labeled data, the quality of a population is assessed through a pseudo-F-measure that relies on heuristic estimates of recall and precision.

HERA [Lin et al., 2020] combines a schema-agnostic similarity with a property alignment scheme. First, it defines as candidate matches the profiles pairs that share at least one attribute value token and the estimated upper bound of their overall similarity exceeds a predetermined threshold. Next, the content similarity of every pair of candidate matches is computed through a schema-agnostic approach that solves a maximum weight matching problem on a bipartite graph. If the similarity exceeds a specific threshold, the two profiles are merged into a "super record" that is used in all their subsequent pairwise comparisons, while their attributes are aligned through a majority voting scheme. This schema information is considered in subsequent comparisons for higher accuracy.

In a different direction, *SERIMI* [Araújo et al., 2015] enhances Matching for Clean-Clean ER by leveraging class information. First, it defines as candidate matches the pairs sharing at least one token in the value of the most distinctive and frequent attribute. Then, for every class of profiles from DS_1, it refines the candidate matches from DS_2 by requiring that they belong to the same class, too. This is achieved by comparing the profiles from DS_2 with each other; those sharing no information with the majority of candidate matches are disregarded. For the retained candidate matches, it estimates the Jaccard similarity on the values of their aligned attributes and requires that it exceeds a specific threshold.

Collective Methods.   As in Generation 1, methods of this type aim to simultaneously disambiguate a set of profiles based on interrelated match decisions.

idMesh [Zhu et al., 2016] performs a probabilistic graph analysis of relations between profile pairs. At its core lies a factor-graph model that captures both matching constraints and trustworthiness of the input DSs. Special care is taken for the temporal discrimination of profiles as well as for the distributed execution of idMesh on top of a shared-nothing infrastructure.

CoSum [Zhu et al., 2016] is crafted for multi-type input DSs. To resolve them, it builds a summary graph that consists of super nodes, which correspond to an entity (i.e., cluster of profiles) and are connected with probabilistically weighted super edges. The algorithm starts with a random summary graph, which is iteratively refined until finding a local optimum with respect to an objective function that depends on the textual and structural similarity of the profiles inside every super node.

Methods for Profile Matching.   Special techniques have been proposed for comparing heterogeneous profile pairs.

Group Linkage [On et al., 2007] is an unsupervised, schema-agnostic approach that represents every profile as a set of values and/or neighbors and transforms a pair-wise comparison into a bipartite graph. Every node corresponds to a set item and every edge connects items of different profiles, weighted according to their similarity. Edges that do not exceed a predetermined threshold ρ are discarded. If the maximum weight bipartite matching exceeds another predetermined threshold θ, the pair of profiles is considered a match. To reduce the high cost of bipartite matching, lower and upper bounds are estimated and used for skipping obvious matches or non-matches, respectively.

Hybrid Field Matcher [Minton et al., 2005] is a domain-specific supervised approach that learns how to compare heterogeneous profiles by normalizing their attribute values. At its core lies on a set of transformations, such as "synonym," and "abbreviation," which form a transformation graph, when applied to a particular profile. The goal is to automatically build the optimal transformation graph for each pair of profiles. This is achieved by a classifier that is trained on a set of positive and negative pairs of attribute values, with those appearing in at least one pair of duplicate profiles considered as positive.

Methods for Executing Matching Rules.   The matching rules learned by the above supervised and unsupervised methods are typically quite complex, involving numerous comparisons of attribute values and different thresholds. To execute them in an efficient way, *HELIOS* [Ngomo, 2014] employs two operators: (i) the rewriter, which produces an equivalent, but faster set of rules and (ii) the planner, which produces the final execution plan.

CONDOR [Georgala et al., 2018] improves the execution of matching rules dynamically, by re-evaluating the original execution plan at run-time. After carrying out the next step in the original plan, it replaces the a-priori estimated costs with the real ones in all considered execution plans. The original plan is altered if the new computations indicate that an alternative one is more efficient for the remaining steps.

5.5   CLUSTERING

As in the previous generations, this step receives as input the similarity graph and produces as output the final set of entities. Unlike the previous generations, though, this step is not optional in Generation 3, unless Matching is performed by supervised methods. Another difference is that the edge weights, i.e., the pairwise similarity scores, are not necessarily extracted from the values of specific attributes. Instead, they typically encapsulate the aggregate similarity of all attribute values in each profile and/or neighbor similarity.

In general, all aforementioned clustering methods are applicable. The only clustering technique that is inherently capable of handling Variety (in the form of heterogeneous semantic types) is *SplitMerge* [Nentwig et al., 2016]. In a nutshell, it applies Connected Components clustering and cleans the resulting clusters by iteratively removing profiles with low similarity to other cluster members. Then, it merges similar clusters that are likely to correspond to the same real-world entity. In this way, SPlitMerge is able to refine the `owl:sameAs` links that are already included in the Linked Open Data cloud, regardless of the entity types that are associated with the corresponding profiles.

5.6   PARALLELIZATION

Not all of the above techniques are able to tackle Volume so as to scale to very large DSs. Hopefully, specialized techniques that address this challenge, together with Veracity and Variety, have been developed for each step in the end-to-end workflow of this generation. We elaborate on the main ones in the following.

5.6.1   BLOCK BUILDING

The MapReduce implementation of the main Block Building methods is presented in Christophides et al. [2015] and Efthymiou et al. [2015b].

Token Blocking builds an inverted index that associates every token with all profiles containing it in their attribute values. This is carried out by a single MapReduce job: for every input profile p_i, the `map` function emits a (t, p_i) pair for every token t in the values of p_i; then, all profiles sharing a particular token are gathered by the same `reduce` function and are placed in the same block.

For the parallelization of Attribute Clustering, four MapReduce jobs are required. The first one assembles all values that correspond to each attribute name. The second job computes the similarities between all attributes, even those placed in different data partitions—an approach similar to the non-approximate algorithm in Zhang et al. [2012] is used for this purpose. The third job associates every attribute with its most similar one. Finally, the fourth job associates every attribute with a cluster id and applies the same process as the MapReduce-based Token Blocking. The only difference is that the `map` function emits pairs of the form $(c_{id}.t, p_i)$, where c_{id} is the cluster id of p_i's attribute that contains token t.

Also complex is the parallelization of Prefix-Infix(-Suffix) Blocking, which involves three MapReduce jobs. The first one parallelizes the algorithm that extracts the prefixes from a set of URIs [Papadakis et al., 2010]. The second one does the same for the extraction of suffixes from a set of URIs. The third job involves two different mappers that run in parallel: (i) the mapper of Token Blocking, which applies to the literal values; and (ii) a specialized mapper, which emits a pair (i, p_i) for every infix i that is extracted from profile's p_i URI, or from the URIs appearing in its values. The final reduce phase ensures that all profiles having a common token or infix in their literals or URIs will be placed in the same block.

5.6.2   BLOCK PROCESSING

Due to their low computational cost, little effort has been devoted on parallelizing block-centric methods for Block Processing. The only exception is the sub-block algorithm in McNeill et al. [2012], which is inherently parallelized on top of the MapReduce framework.

Block Filtering has been adapted to the MapReduce framework in Efthymiou et al. [2015a]. The adaptation requires a single job, where the Map function iterates over the input blocks to emit key-value pairs of the form key = "profile id," value = "block_id.block_cardinality." The Reduce function receives all block ids per profile, sorts them in ascending cardinality and retains the first r%.

Due to its higher computational cost, more effort has been devoted to parallelizing Meta-blocking on top of MapReduce. Three alternative strategies have been proposed in Efthymiou et al. [2017].

1. The *edge-based strategy* builds the blocking graph *explicitly*, storing all the edges along with their weights on the disk. This bears a significant I/O cost that becomes the bottleneck for very large blocking graphs.

2. The *comparison-based strategy* offers a more efficient implementation that builds the blocking graph *implicitly*. A pre-processing job enriches every block with the list of block ids associated with every one of its profiles. Thus, every edge weight is computed *locally* by the Map function of the next job. This function identifies and ignores all redundant comparisons, reducing significantly the number of edges that are stored on the disk. This is the most efficient strategy for the edge-centric pruning schemes, namely WEP and CEP, as it minimizes the required number of MapReduce jobs. Indeed, two jobs are required for pruning the superfluous comparisons. The first one estimates the pruning threshold, while the second one applies it.

3. The *entity-based strategy* is independent of the blocking graph. It aggregates for every profile the bag of all profiles that co-occur with it in at least one block. Then, it estimates the edge weight that corresponds to each neighbor based on its frequency in the co-occurrence bag. This is the most efficient strategy for the node-centric pruning schemes (i.e., WNP,

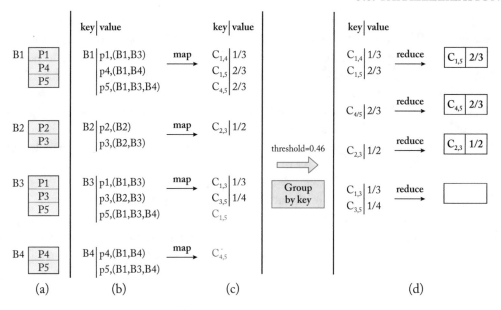

Figure 5.9: Applying the comparison-based strategy for WEP: (a) the initial set of blocks; (b) the corresponding key-value pairs obtained by the pre-processing step; and (c) the output of the `map` function with the comparison ids as keys and the corresponding Jaccard similarity of the block lists as weight, and (d) the `reduce` phase.

CNP and their variations), since both edge weighting and edge pruning are carried out within the Reduce function of a single job, minimizing the I/O overhead.

Example 5.5   Figure 5.9 illustrates the comparison-based strategy for parallelizing WEP. The initial set of blocks is shown in Figure 5.9a. The `map` function receives as input the key-value pairs of Figure 5.9b: the keys correspond to the block ids and the values to the profile ids in the block along with the ids of all blocks that contain every profile. For every non-redundant comparison in the block, the mapper outputs the id of the comparison as key (e.g., $c1.4$ for the profile pair p_1-p_4) and the corresponding weight as value, as shown in Figure 5.9c. In this case, the Jaccard similarity is used as the weighting scheme, i.e., the weight of every edge is equal to the number of blocks shared by the adjacent candidate matches divided by the number of distinct blocks they belong to. Redundant comparisons are shown in red. The reduce step is illustrated in Figure 5.9d, where only pairs with a weight above the average one (≈ 0.46) are emitted. Thus, the comparisons $c_{1,4}$, $c_{1,3}$, and $c_{3,5}$ are pruned.

To avoid the underutilization of the available resources, a specialized algorithm for Load Balancing, *MaxBlock*, was introduced in Efthymiou et al. [2017]. It exploits the highly skewed distribution of sizes in redundancy-positive sets of blocks in order to split them in partitions of equivalent computational cost (i.e., total number of comparisons). This computational cost is determined by the comparisons of the largest input block. MaxBlock fits easily to the limited memory that is available in each node, due to its *optimized representation model*: every profile is represented by an integer that denotes its id, while every block consists of a list of integers and is itself identified by a unique integer id. The same representation is used by all parallelization strategies described above.

Another approach to parallelizing Meta-blocking is the *multi-core execution* [Papadakis et al., 2017], which makes the most of the available processors in a stand-alone system. The key idea is to split the overall computational cost into a set of chunks that are placed in an array, with an index indicating the next chunk to be processed. Following the established fork-join model, every thread retrieves the current value of the index and is assigned to process corresponding chunk.

5.6.3   MATCHING

LINDA [Böhm et al., 2012] and MinoanER [Efthymiou et al., 2019] are implemented in MapReduce by default. For LINDA, every cluster node retains part of the priority queue along with the corresponding profile sub-graph, performing local computations in every iteration. Similarly, every worker in MinoanER contains the part of the blocking graph that is necessary to find the match of a specific profile. The execution of the matching rules is interleaved as much as possible so as to minimize the running time.

Example 5.6   Figure 5.10 illustrates LINDA's functionality in the context of a two-node MapReduce cluster, when applied to the Knowledge Bases in Figures 5.8a and b. The priority queue is divided into two partitions, with each one assigned to a different node, as shown in Figure 5.10b. Each node also gets a partition of the entity graph with all profiles in its local priority queue as well as their immediate neighbors. This is depicted in Figure 5.10a. Figure 5.10c illustrates the sequence of tasks occurring when the profiles $A2$ and $B2$ are designated as duplicates. These tasks, which are highlighted in pink, are the following: (1) the associated mapper updates the result matrix; (2) the same mapper sends notification messages to share the new matching evidence; and (3) the reducer reacts to the received messages in order to emit similarity score updates for the graph neighbors of the associated profiles, as well as any required updates to the local priority queues.

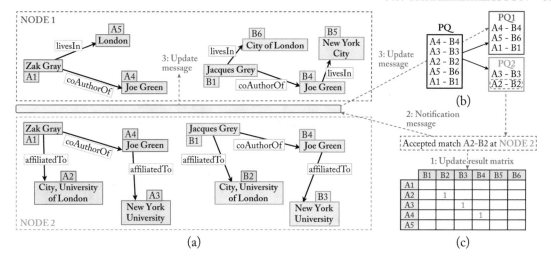

Figure 5.10: Applying LINDA to the Knowledge Bases in Figures 5.8a and b within a two-node MapReduce cluster: (a) partitions of the entity graph resulting from the priority queue partitioning, (b) partitions of the original priority queue; and (c) the sequence of tasks after a new pair of duplicates is detected.

5.6.4 CLUSTERING

SplitMerge is adapted to the MapReduce implementation of Apache Flink in Nentwig et al. [2017a], based on Gelly, Flink's graph-processing API. Similar to the serial processing, the parallel one consists of four consecutive steps. In each step, one or more operators of Flink and Gelly are employed for the distributed processing. This approach can be adapted to Apache Spark,[2] too.

[2]https://spark.apache.org

CHAPTER 6

Generation 4: Also Addressing Velocity

This generation differs from the previous ones in two aspects:

1. there are time constraints with respect to the ER running time; and

2. the volume of input data increases continuously with time, a challenge known as *Velocity*.

The input ranges from structured data to semi-structured ones, even data lakes. In the latter case, Variety is also present, whereas Volume and Veracity are intrinsic characteristics in all cases.

When the time constraints are relatively loose, in the order of minutes or even hours, the goal is to provide best possible *partial solution* within the required response time. This task, called **Budget-aware** or **Progressive ER** [Papenbrock et al., 2015, Simonini et al., 2019, Whang et al., 2013b], is addressed by *pay-as-you-go* applications that do not require the complete solution to produce useful results, due to the unprecedented, increasing volume of available data. For example, there are 233 million Web tables[1] and 26 billion datasets indexed by the Google search engine [Golshan et al., 2017, Halevy et al., 2016]; these datasets can only be resolved progressively [Golshan et al., 2017]. We describe the relevant techniques in Section 6.1.

Example 6.1 Figure 6.1 provides a high-level description of Progressive Entity Resolution. The horizontal axis corresponds to running time, with three different points in time marked on it such that $t_1 < t_2 < t_3$ and $t_3 - t_2 \approx t_2 - t_1$. At all times, the input comprises the same data, DS_1 and DS_2, which are both clean. At t_1, very few comparisons are executed between the profiles of the two DSs. Thus, the number of detected duplicates is also low, albeit high in relation to the number of comparisons (i.e., high precision). As we move to t_2 and t_3, the number of comparisons and detected duplicates increase almost analogously. That is, precision remains relatively stable so that recall depends almost linearly on the available time budget.

When the time constraints are strict, the task is called **Real-time ER** [Christen et al., 2009, Ramadan and Christen, 2014], **Query-based ER** [Altwaijry et al., 2015, 2017, Bhattacharya and Getoor, 2007b], **Online ER** [Karapiperis et al., 2018a], or **Incremental ER** [Gruenheid et al., 2014]. The input comprises a stream of query profiles that have to be individually

---
[1]http://webdatacommons.org/webtables/2015/relationalStatistics.html

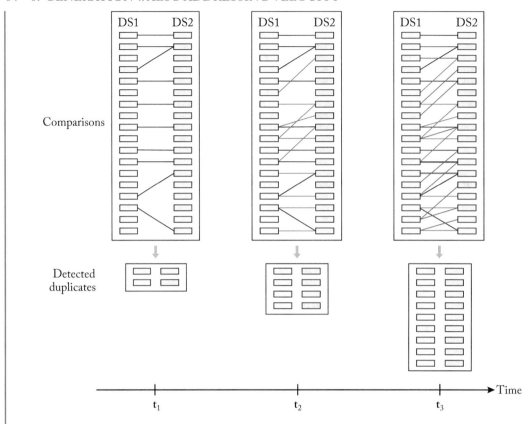

Figure 6.1: Generic outline of Progressive ER.

resolved over a large DS in the shortest possible time (ideally at sub-second latency) and perhaps with a minimum memory footprint. In these settings, resolving the whole input DSs is unnecessarily costly in terms of time and resources. Instead, only a fraction of the stored profiles that are most similar to the query should be considered. As an example, consider an application used by a journalist to associate every profile extracted from a stream of news articles and social media posts with additional information from a data lake. We describe the main relevant techniques in Section 6.2.

Example 6.2 A high-level description of Incremental ER is given in Figure 6.2. Again, the horizontal axis corresponds to time, with three points in time marked on it: $t_1 < t_2 < t_3$. At t_1, an ER approach is applied to the input DS to derive the respective set of entities. At t_2, the input DS is enriched with new profiles, which are highlighted in green. The goal of Incremental ER is to match these new profiles against the old ones (and against each other) without performing all brute-force comparisons. Instead, it minimizes the old profiles that are involved in this process,

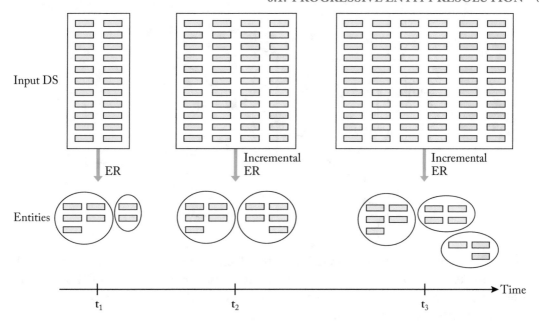

Figure 6.2: Generic outline of Incremental ER.

restricting the computational cost to the most similar or affected profiles. The same applies to the new profiles arriving at t_3, which are marked in blue. Along with the cost minimization, special care is taken to update and refine the initial entities in view of the new similarity evidence. This is demonstrated at t_3, where the circle corresponding to the rightmost entity comprises one of the profiles of the rightmost entity at t_2.

6.1   PROGRESSIVE ENTITY RESOLUTION

This type of ER serves applications with a limited budget of computational and/or temporal resources, e.g., in case a large, powerful cluster is only available for a couple of hours. In such cases, the goal is to optimize the processing order of the input data so as to detect as many duplicates as early as possible—unlike **batch/budget-agnostic ER**, shown in previous generations, which produces results in no particular order. The difference between batch and progressive approaches, when applied to the same input data, is formalized by two requirements [Whang et al., 2013b].

- *Same eventual quality.* Both should produce the same results at time t_2, which is the time required by the batch approach to process all input data.

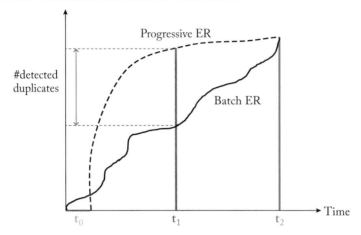

Figure 6.3: The rate of detecting duplicates for batch and progressive ER. The vertical double-arrow illustrates the added benefit of progressive ER when compared to batch ER, i.e., the additional duplicates that progressive ER has detected at time t_1, when compared to the duplicates detected by batch ER within the same processing time.

- *Improved early quality.* At any time $t_1 < t_2$, the batch approach should detect a lower number of duplicates than the progressive one. The lower t_1 is, the higher the difference of the two approaches should be.

These requirements are illustrated in Figure 6.3, where the horizontal axis corresponds to the running time, while the vertical one measures the number of detected duplicates. As a result, the area under the curve of each approach represents its *rate of detecting duplicates*; the higher it is, the more effective is the corresponding method in detecting matches as early as possible. Note, though, that there is a delay in the responses of the progressive approach: the first matches are only produced after time t_0, as shown in Figure 6.3. This is actually the *initialization time*, which is taken to schedule the processing order of blocks, profiles or comparisons.

Depending on the presence of Variety, there are two different end-to-end pipelines for Progressive ER.

1. The *schema-aware workflow*, which is depicted in Figure 6.4a, is suitable only for structured data that is described by a homogeneous schema. It seems similar to the 1st- and 2nd-generation workflows (see Figure 3.1), but is fundamentally different in two respects: (i) a new step, called *Prioritization*, intervenes between Blocking and Matching; and (ii) blocking has become an optional step, because some Prioritization methods apply directly to the input data.

2. The *schema-agnostic workflow*, which appears in Figure 6.4b, is inherently crafted for highly heterogeneous (semi-)structured data. It extends the 3rd-generation workflow in Fig-

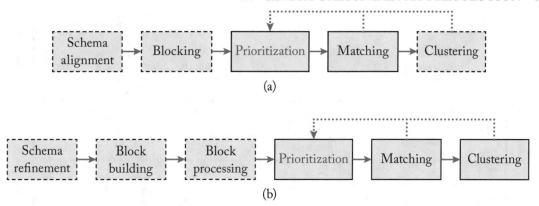

Figure 6.4: (a) The schema-aware and (b) the schema-agnostic versions of the 4th generation of the end-to-end ER workflow. Dashed contours indicate optional steps.

ure 5.1 in two ways: (i) it adds Prioritization between Block Processing and Matching; and (ii) it turns Block Building into an optional step that is useful only in case the selected Prioritization method does not apply directly to the input DS(s).

Except Prioritization, all other steps have been analytically described in the earlier generations. For this reason, we exclusively discuss Prioritization techniques in the following.

6.1.1 PRIORITIZATION

The input to this step comprises a set of blocks or profiles. Internally, Prioritization processes this input and assigns a weight to all profiles, comparisons or blocks in order to schedule their processing in decreasing likelihood that they involve duplicates. Then, the top-weighted profile pairs are iteratively emitted, one at a time, to apply the Matching (and Clustering) algorithm to their profiles.

We distinguish Prioritization into two main categories, depending on its relation to Matching.

1. The *static progressive techniques* produce an immutable processing order independently of Matching.

2. The *dynamic progressive techniques* rely on the feedback from the outcome of profile comparisons, i.e., whether they involve duplicates or not, so as to adjust the original processing order on-the-fly. This is illustrated by the dotted lines from Matching and Clustering to Prioritization in Figures 6.4a and b.

Below, we delve into the methods of each category.

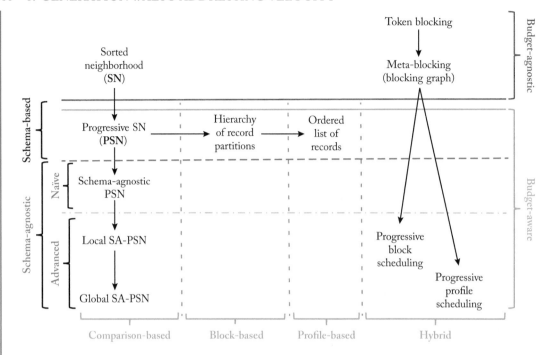

Figure 6.5: The two-dimensional taxonomy of the main static Progressive ER methods formed by the granularity of their functionality (horizontal axis) and their schema-awareness (vertical axis), based on Simonini et al. [2019].

Static Progressive Methods.   The majority of Prioritization algorithms involves a static processing that is independent of Matching. These methods are organized in a two-dimensional categorization that is depicted in Figure 6.5. The horizontal axis corresponds to the *granularity of functionality*, i.e., the items that are weighted in proportion to the likelihood that they involve duplicates. These items are then processed in decreasing order, from the most likely match to the least one. Four subcategories are defined:

1. the comparison-based methods, which weight pairs of profiles,

2. the block-based methods, which assign weights to each block,

3. the entity-based methods, which assign weights to every individual profile, and

4. the hybrid methods, which combine characteristics from at least two of the previous categories.

   The vertical axis corresponds to *schema-awareness*. The earlier progressive methods were schema-based, in the sense that schema knowledge was crucial for their functionality. In Whang

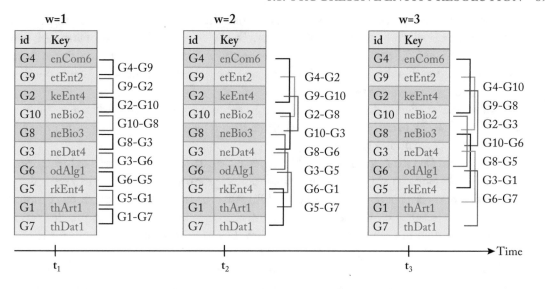

Figure 6.6: Applying Progressive Sorted Neighborhood to the DS in Figure 2.2 using the blocking keys of Example 3.3 and Figure 3.4. The pairs of profiles indicate the comparisons that are executed in every iteration as a result of the corresponding sliding window w.

et al. [2013b], a representative schema-based method is presented for each level of granularity, except the hybrid one.

Progressive Sorted Neighborhood (PSN) is a comparison-based approach that leverages the sorted list of profiles formed by Sorted Neighborhood [Hernández and Stolfo, 1995]. Initially, it compares all profiles in consecutive positions through a sliding window of size $w = 1$, starting from the top of the list. Then, all profiles at distance $w = 2$ are compared and so on and so forth, until termination.

Example 6.3   Figure 6.6 illustrates an example of applying PSN to the DS of Figure 2.2. The blocking keys of Example 3.3 and Figure 3.4 are sorted in alphabetical order along with the associated profile ids. Each point in time corresponds to a different window size w, which increases gradually so as to progressively compare profiles in a longer distance. At t_1, pairs of profiles in consecutive positions are examined ($w = 1$), starting from the top of the sorted list. At times t_2 and t_3, the window size is incremented to $w = 2$ and $w = 3$, respectively, with the processing starting again from the top of sorted list.

Hierarchy of Record Partitions [Whang et al., 2013b] is a block-based approach that builds a tree of blocks such that the matching likelihood of two profiles is proportional to the level in which they co-occur for the first time; the most likely matches are placed in the leaves, while nodes at higher levels correspond to less likely matches. The resulting tree is then progressively resolved, level by level, from the leaves to the root. To clarify how this tree is constructed, consider as an example l different edit distance thresholds for the similarity of the schema-based blocking keys, where l is the number of levels in the tree; the smallest threshold corresponds to the leaves, and the largest one to the root.

For higher efficiency, a variation of this approach is adapted to MapReduce in Altowim and Mehrotra [2017]: every block is divided into a hierarchy of child blocks that are optimally processed through a complex strategy.

Finally, the *Ordered List of Records* [Whang et al., 2013b] converts the tree of blocks into a list of profiles that are sorted in descending likelihood to produce matches. This can be achieved by associating every level in the tree with a probability that the corresponding partition of profiles is the actual ER result, i.e., the correct set of entities. The resulting order of profiles can be seamlessly integrated into any Matching algorithm, but in practice its effectiveness is slightly lower than that of the Hierarchy of Record Partitions.

The rest of the progressive methods are *schema-agnostic*, tackling Variety by disregarding completely any schema knowledge. We can distinguish them into two broad categories [Simonini et al., 2019].

1. The *sort-based methods* extend PSN, relying on the proximity of blocking keys in the alphabetical order.

2. The *hash-based methods* extract the optimal processing order from the edge weights of Meta-blocking, i.e., from the co-occurrence patterns in a hash-based, redundancy-positive set of blocks.

Among the sort-based methods, *Schema-agnostic PSN* [Simonini et al., 2019] simply replaces the schema-based blocking key of PSN with the schema-agnostic ones, i.e., all attribute value tokens [Papadakis et al., 2015]. This means that no human intervention is required for applying it to the input data. On the downsize, every profile is associated with multiple keys and, thus, appears multiple times in the ordered list of entities. As a result, the sliding window yields redundant comparisons, while the profiles with identical keys are ordered in an arbitrary way. Schema-agnostic PSN is incapable of addressing these issues, thus being a naive approach.

In contrast, *Local Schema-agnostic PSN* [Simonini et al., 2019] addresses these issues by leveraging the co-occurrence patterns of profile pairs in the current window size w. Every distinct pair of profiles at distance w is weighted in proportion to its frequency, which is normalized by the number of positions per profile. In this way, all redundant comparisons are eliminated and the rest are sorted in descending weights.

However, this approach does not prevent some pairs from re-appearing in different window sizes, still yielding redundant comparisons. To overcome this issue, *Global Schema-agnostic PSN* [Simonini et al., 2019] weights all distinct pairs within a specific range of window sizes.

Among the hash-based methods, the naive approach is to use directly the comparison weights produced by Meta-blocking. Indeed, we can order in decreasing weight the top-K edges of the entire blocking graph or per node (profile), where K is estimated according to the available resources [Papadakis et al., 2020a].

For a more accurate processing order, *Progressive Profile Scheduling* [Simonini et al., 2019] involves a hybrid functionality that combines comparison and profile weights in order to optimize the processing order of the given profiles. It estimates the average comparison weight per profile, assuming that the higher it is, the more likely is the corresponding profile to be matching with one or more others. Then, it sorts all profiles in decreasing average weight and starts its processing from the top weighted one. For each profile, it sorts its comparisons in decreasing weight and starts from the top-weighted one.

Progressive Block Scheduling [Simonini et al., 2019] minimizes the initialization time by combining block and comparison weights. Based on the assumption of many Block Processing techniques that smaller blocks are more likely to contain duplicates, it first orders all blocks in increasing size or cardinality. Then, it starts from the first (smallest) block, processing its comparisons in decreasing edge weight, and so on and so forth, until consuming the available budget.

Dynamic Progressive Methods.   Dynamic variations of schema-based techniques have been proposed in Papenbrock et al. [2015], assuming that Matching is carried out by a perfect oracle, which decides with 100% accuracy whether two profiles are matching or not. Dynamic PSN arranges the sorted profiles in a two-dimensional array A such that if $A(i, j)$ corresponds to a duplicate, the processing moves on to check $A(i + 1, j)$ and $A(i, j + 1)$, as well. Similarly, *Progressive Blocking* starts by arranging the blocks of Standard Blocking in a two-dimensional array A. Then, it executes all comparisons inside every block, measuring the number of duplicates per block. If the block with the highest density of duplicates corresponds to $A(i, j)$, its profiles are compared with those in $A(i + 1, j)$ and $A(i, j + 1)$ so as to detect more matches.

A schema-agnostic dynamic approach is pBlocking [Galhotra et al., 2020], which essentially augments a blocking workflow so that it considers the feedback of Matching. The blocking workflow consists of one or more Block Building techniques, which create a hierarchy of small blocks, and two Block Processing methods: a block-centric one, which assigns scores to individual blocks and prunes those below a threshold; and a meta-blocking approach for pruning individual comparisons. After applying Matching to the smallest blocks, intersections of the initial blocks are formed and scored based on their ratio of duplicate and non-duplicate profiles as well as on the diversity of their profiles. Next, meta-blocking is applied. This process is iteratively applied until convergence. pBlocking's high effectiveness and time efficiency are experimentally and theoretically verified.

On another line of research, a progressive solution for collective matching methods for is presented in Altowim et al. [2014]. Based on a graph representation that is similar to DepG-graph [Dong et al., 2005], it operates in two levels: first, it partitions the budget into windows of the same cost and then, it prioritizes the comparisons inside every window based on a cost-benefit formula. After processing every window, the match decisions are propagated to all affected profile pairs through the graph representation.

6.2   INCREMENTAL ENTITY RESOLUTION

The end-to-end workflow for Incremental ER is the same as Generations 1 and 2, depicted in Figure 3.1, given that all techniques are schema-based, assuming as input structured data with aligned schemata. Yet, the methods of these generations are inapplicable to Velocity settings, as they assume a static data collection as input. All workflow steps thus call for novel techniques that are inherently capable of dynamically adapting to the incoming data. Below, we present the main techniques for each workflow step.

Methods for Incremental Schema Matching.   This task was introduced in Franklin et al. [2005], which coined the notion of Dataspaces, where heterogeneous data of different formats co-exist without requiring any semantic integration of their schemata prior to receiving and answering queries. Instead, the schemata are integrated in a query-driven way that improves its results incrementally, as more query profiles arrive.

iTrails [Salles et al., 2007] exploits "hints" about partial schema knowledge to gradually create a global schema, while a boot-strapping approach is presented in Sarma et al. [2008]. Its goal is to automatically create probabilistic links between the individual schemata and a mediated one that will constitute the starting point for incremental schema matching and will be later refined.

The search system in Madhavan et al. [2007] uses a set of mechanisms that continuously resolve and improve the schema over time. It incorporates implicit feedback as well as explicit help from users. The former is done by processing the reactions of the users over the profiles returned as results (i.e., by monitoring the selected query answers), while the latter is retrieved through questions to the users, asking them if the returned profiles are relevant.

Methods for Incremental Blocking.   Their goal is to maintain a *dynamic* set of blocks such that the contents of individual blocks are updated as new profiles arrive, while minimizing the time required for detecting the likely matches per query.

The *local* incremental blocking methods include the earliest relevant technique, which precalculates the similarities between the profiles that co-occur in the blocks of Standard Blocking [Christen et al., 2009]. Thus, no similarity computations are required at query time, minimizing the query response time.

DySimII [Ramadan et al., 2013] updates all three indexes as query profiles arrive, while maintaining practically stable their average record insertion and query times, despite the increase in the index size.

The *global* incremental methods mainly extend schema-aware Sorted Neighborhood. *F-DySNI* [Ramadan and Christen, 2014, Ramadan et al., 2015] converts the alphabetically ordered list of blocking keys into a braided AVL tree [Rice, 2007] that provides quick search. This tree combines a height-balanced binary tree with a double-linked list, where every node is linked to its predecessor and successor nodes as well as to the list of all profile ids that correspond to its blocking key. There is a separate tree for every blocking key definition, with all trees getting updated whenever a query profile arrives.

F-DySNI is extended in Ramadan and Christen [2015] with an algorithm for automatically selecting the blocking keys of Sorted Neighborhood. This algorithm combines the weak training set of FisherDisjunctive [Kejriwal and Miranker, 2013] with a scoring function that for each candidate key assesses how high is its coverage and how low are the average block size and the variance of block sizes.

Another global incremental method is CF-RDS [Karapiperis et al., 2018b], which is based on Hamming LSH. Upon receiving a query profile p, it identifies the buckets associated with it and gathers the profiles they contain at the moment. Instead of comparing them with p, it ranks them in descending order of frequency in these buckets.

Example 6.4   Figure 6.7 illustrates an example of applying F-DySNI to the DS of Figure 2.2, with profile G10 being the query profile. Attributes "Affiliation" and "Areas of Interest" are used to form blocking keys from their entire values. The resulting sorted lists are shown in Figure 6.7a. The AVL tree structures, which are illustrated in Figure 6.7b, facilitate the candidate retrieval process: each node represents a key value and the profiles associated with it are shown in blue below it. Blue and dashed arrows are links to alphabetically sorted predecessor and successor nodes, respectively. The fixed window, $w = 2$, indicates the number of neighboring nodes that are considered in each direction to generate the matching candidates. In the upper tree, three nodes are thus considered: the node that includes the new entry and the two neighboring ones to its right (they are pointed with green arrows). They are associated with the profiles G3, G9, and G4 and generate the comparisons shown in red at the top of Figure 6.7c.

In the lower tree, a new key "Bioinformatics" must be inserted for $G10$ between "Artificial Intelligence," "Text mining," and "Biological Databases." The fixed window now covers four nodes, two at the left and two at the right of the new entry. The corresponding matching candidates are shown in red at the bottom of Figure 6.7c.

A *hybrid* blocking approach blends MinHash LSH with Sorted Neighborhood in Liang et al. [2014]. When searching for the nearest neighbors of a query, the profiles in large LSH blocks are sorted via a custom scoring function and a fixed-size window slides over the resulting sorted list.

On another line of research, *BlockSketch* [Karapiperis et al., 2018a] ensures bounded matching time by summarizing an individual block b_i so that it suffices to compare every query with a fixed number of profiles from b_i. **S***BlockSketch* [Karapiperis et al., 2018a] adapts *BlockS-*

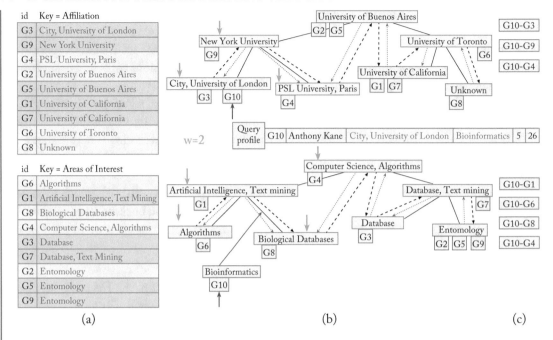

Figure 6.7: Applying F-DySNI with fixed window size $w = 2$ to the DS in Figure 2.2: (a) The two sorted list of blocking keys, which are extracted from the attributes "Affiliation" and "Areas of Interest," (b) the AVL trees for each key, and (c) the set of matching candidates derived from each tree for the query profile G10.

ketch so that it handles potentially unbounded streaming data with a constant amount of main memory.

Methods for Incremental Matching.   We can distinguish the methods of this category according to the type of queries they target.

Simple selection queries are answered by *RC-ER* [Bhattacharya and Getoor, 2007b] through a two-stage approach. First, it retrieves the relevant profiles for each query using two expansion operators, and then, it resolves these profiles collectively, as in Bhattacharya and Getoor [2007a].

Simple selection queries over multiple Web data sources are answered by *UDD* [Su et al., 2010] in an unsupervised way. First, it gathers the results from all sources and marks as non-matches those of the same origin. The resulting labeled dataset is used for training two cooperating classifiers, which iteratively detect duplicates in the query results.

Aggregate numerical queries over voluminous DSs are answered by *SampleClean* [Wang et al., 2014]. A small data sample is resolved and then used to provide approximate responses.

SQL-like selection queries over a single DS are answered by *QDA* [Altwaijry et al., 2017]. Its goal is to minimize the comparisons that must be executed in order to identify all entities in a given block that satisfy the selection predicate. Every block is transformed into a blocking graph and, based on cliques, it detects and discards *vestigial edges*, i.e., comparisons that can be skipped without any impact on the quality of the end result. For example, given two Clean DSs, a comparison is vestigial if p_i or p_j or both of them have already been matched to some other profile and, thus, they cannot be duplicates.

Complex join queries over multiple, overlapping, dirty DSs are answered by *QuERy* [Altwaijry et al., 2015]. It detects which pairs of blocks should be joined, resolving their contents through a black-box matching algorithm. It leverages vestigiality and can be combined with QDA for higher efficiency [Altwaijry et al., 2017].

Queries under data uncertainty are answered by *EAQP* [Ioannou et al., 2010]. The attribute values of each profile are associated with a degree of uncertainty that reflects the noise of an imperfect information extractor. Probabilities are also assigned to profile pairs, indicating their matching likelihood. Each query is answered by merging the matching profiles with the minimum uncertainty among all possible worlds.

Entity uncertainty is also considered by *RAQA* [Sismanis et al., 2009], which answers group-by, roll-up and drill-down Online Analytical Processing (OLAP) queries. Despite maintaining the input DSs unresolved, it returns a strict range of possible values over all possible resolution results along with an indication of whether a cell is guaranteed to be consistently nonempty or not.

On another line of research, Whang and Garcia-Molina [2010] examines Incremental ER in the context of evolving matching rules. The goal is to leverage existing, materialized ER results so as to save the cost of running the ER algorithm from scratch over all input data. The authors prove theoretically that if the ER algorithm satisfies several properties, the results can be updated in a significantly lower runtime. These theoretical properties are extended in Whang and Garcia-Molina [2014] to cover evolving data, too.

Finally, a stream of product descriptions from Web data sources is incrementally resolved in Bilenko et al. [2005]. Using online learning, a composite similarity function is incrementally trained, achieving both high effectiveness and scalability.

Methods for Incremental Clustering.   Several algorithms aim to maintain the entities detected by Correlation Clustering, as more profiles arrive over time. Some are crafted for a fixed number of clusters [Charikar et al., 2004, Mathieu et al., 2010], while others support an unconstrained functionality, with an open number of clusters [Gruenheid et al., 2014]. In the latter case, all possible kinds of updates are supported, such as enriching an entity with new profiles or splitting an entire entity into smaller ones. Special care is also taken to correct past errors in view of new evidence.

Two algorithms for Incremental Multi-source ER are proposed in Saeedi et al. [2020]. *Max-Both Merge* creates a new edge for every pair of profiles that stem from different DSs and are mutually the most similar ones. If one of the profiles/nodes is located into an existing (equivalence) cluster c, the new edge is merged into c as long as c contains at most one profile per DS. Otherwise, a new cluster is created. As a result, this approach depends on the order the new profiles arrive. To address this issue, *n-Depth Reclustering* selects the clusters that are associated with the new profiles along with their neighboring clusters that are at most n edges away. These clusters are then processed by a batch algorithm, namely CLIP (see Section 3.4).

CHAPTER 7

Leveraging External Knowledge

During the last few years, *External Knowledge* was shown to be an extremely interesting mechanism that improves the accuracy of the final set of discovered entities. Hence, methods using external knowledge lie at the focus of the latest resolution breakthroughs. We group the related methods into two categories/sections. Section 7.1 describes methods that use DL techniques, incorporating contextual information in the form of pre-trained word or character embeddings or transformer-based language models. Section 7.2 describes ER methods that use crowdsourcing, relying on human feedback as the external knowledge.

7.1 DEEP LEARNING

DL is a subfield of Machine Learning that focuses on learning multiple levels of representation using complex neural networks [Goodfellow et al., 2016]. In essence, it teaches computers to learn by example, which is something that comes naturally to humans. The basic idea is that if you provide a neural network with tons of information, it will begin to understand it and respond in useful ways.

DL has transformed many fields, such as Computer Vision, Speech Recognition, and Natural Language Processing [Goodfellow et al., 2016]. Given the recent breakthrough of DL in various fields, a bulk of works examine their application in most steps of the end-to-end ER workflows. The resulting learning-based techniques differ from those of the previous generations in two respects.

1. They go beyond hand-crafted, dataset-specific features, which require an expensive, time-consuming process. Instead, they automatically learn complex, dataset- and domain-agnostic features. Most works actually leverage **embeddings**, which are dense, multi-dimensional vectors representing a word or character n-gram that have been pre-trained over large, generic corpora such as Wikipedia.[1] As a result, these methods capture domain-agnostic, *external* knowledge that is independent of a particular ER task.

2. These methods employ various forms of **Deep Neural Networks** as classification algorithms or simply summarization mechanisms. Their complex architectures enable them to

---

[1]https://www.wikipedia.org

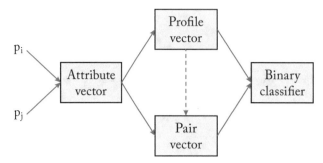

Figure 7.1: The general methodology of DL-based ER methods.

improve their effectiveness in proportion to the size of the training data. This is in contrast to traditional machine learning algorithms that reach a plateau of effectiveness after few million profiles.

In this context, the DL-based methods generally follow the methodology that is illustrated in Figure 7.1. Initially, the textual value of an individual attribute is converted into a dense feature vector using embeddings (see below). This sequence of vectors is summarized into an *attribute vector* with a simple operator (e.g., addition, substraction, or multiplication) or more often through a deep neural network. The latter case typically involves variants of recurrent neural networks (**RNNs**), which are specialized for processing sequences of inputs, as their neurons are fed information not only from the previous layer, but also from their own previous state in time. The most popular forms are the long short-term memory (**LSTM**) and the bidirectional gated recurrent unit (**BiGRU**) networks. For more details, please refer to Goodfellow et al. [2016]. Attention mechanisms might be employed, too, either in isolation or in combination with RNNs, in order to emphasize the most important items in profile vectors. The resulting set of attribute vectors is combined into a *profile vector* with simple operations like concatenation or through an RNN summarization. In the simplest case, the profile vectors of two candidate matches are fed to a *binary classifier*, which typically constitutes a variant of Multi-layer Perceptron (**MLP**) in combination with softmax [Barlaug and Gulla, 2020]. Alternatively, two profile vectors first yield a *pair vector* through a simple function, such as cosine similarity or Euclidean distance, or through a learnable function, such as element-wise absolute difference or multiplication [Mudgal et al., 2018]. The pair vector, which can be formed directly from the attribute vectors of the compared profiles, is then fed to a binary classifier.

Embeddings.   Every textual attribute value is typically considered as a sequence of items, which are tokens (i.e., words) or character n-grams, of arbitrary length. Every item is converted into a dense feature vector through embeddings. Depending on their granularity, they are distinguished into Mudgal et al. [2018]:

1. *word-level embeddings*, such as word2vec [Mikolov et al., 2013] and GloVe [Pennington et al., 2014]; and

2. *character-level embeddings*, such as fastText [Bojanowski et al., 2017].

Depending on their origin, they are distinguished into Mudgal et al. [2018]:

1. *learned embeddings*, which are locally trained over the available labeled data, producing domain-specific embeddings; and

2. *pre-trained embeddings*, which have been extracted from global, large and generic corpora with unsupervised learning. They eliminate the training time, while capturing a large variety of patterns.

Note that the pre-trained word-level embeddings are inappropriate for highly specialized ER tasks, which involve domain-specific tokens that are not included in the training corpora of word2vec and GloVe. For example, product names usually involve arbitrary alphanumerics with no particular meaning (e.g., $i7$), while bibliographic data abound in venue acronyms, such as SIGMOD or VLDB. These cases are called *out-of-vocabulary tokens* and are typically mapped to a special token like UNK that corresponds to a default embedding vector. This means that different words end up with the same vector, thus leading to lower accuracy. Hopefully, character-level pre-trained embeddings can overcome this issue: fastText vectorizes a token by summing the embeddings of all its n-grams.

In general, the embeddings are quite effective in capturing the semantic relatedness of two terms, e.g., "queen" and "king." However, the pre-trained embeddings capture relationships that are valid in the training corpora, but do not hold in the case of the data they are applied to, e.g., the fact that "Steve" and "Apple" are close might not be true on a particular use case. The opposite is also true: the pre-trained embeddings do not capture patterns that exist in the testing data, but are absent from the training corpora. In general, they do not perform well with attribute values that lack a semantic meaning, such as numeric values, person names, and birth dates.

Unlike these shallow embeddings, which are usually trained to predict the next word, the *transformer-based language models*, namely *BERT* [Devlin et al., 2019] and its variants, are trained to predict a masked token when knowing its left and right context. In this way, they capture contextual information that enables them to distinguish *homonyms* and *synonyms*. The former correspond to words that have the same form, but different meaning (e.g., the word "bank" refers to a financial institution or the border of a river). The shallow, context-agnostic models assign the same vector to both meanings, unlike the transformer-based models, which rely on the context in order to identify the right vector. The opposite happens with synonyms, which are different words with the same meaning (e.g., "enormous" and "vast").

7.1.1   SCHEMA MATCHING

Several approaches leverage pre-trained embeddings in order to boost the effectiveness of Schema Matching.

The simplest one is presented in Nozaki et al. [2019]: for every attribute, all its values are aggregated and each one is converted into an instance vector by summing the word2vec vectors of its tokens/words. Out of vocabulary cases are simply ignored. Attribute vectors are then constructed by averaging the corresponding instance vectors. Finally, cosine similarity is applied to all pairs of attribute vectors and those exceeding a specific threshold indicate semantically equivalent attributes.

LEAPME [Hernández et al., 2020] is a similar, yet supervised, approach that is crafted for Multi-source ER. In this case, the instance vectors complement the average of Glove word embeddings with meta-features, such as the portion and the frequency of numeric, lowercase, and uppercase characters. The attribute vectors concatenate the average of instance vectors with the average embedding vector of the words forming the attribute name. A property pair vector is then formed for every pair of attributes by subtracting the corresponding attribute vectors and adding string similarity scores, e.g., the edit distance of attribute names. These vectors are then fed to a neural network which is trained over labeled data from some of the input DSs.

Finally, *SemProp* [Fernandez et al., 2018] is a complex, unsupervised approach that uses two types of attribute matchers: (i) syntactic ones, which consider the textual similarity of instances (i.e., attribute values) and attribute names; and (ii) semantic ones, which rely on the concept of coherent groups, i.e., clusters of words for which the average cosine similarity of their embedding vectors is higher than a specific threshold. The evidence from these two matchers is combined with structural evidence in order to produce the final set of matching attributes.

7.1.2   BLOCKING

Two methods have been proposed for blocking, *DeepER* [Ebraheem et al., 2018] and *Auto-Block* [Zhang et al., 2020b]. Both are schema-aware, thus corresponding to Generation 1, and implement the same approach in principle: they create a high-dimensional vector representation for every profile based on pre-trained embeddings and cast blocking as a nearest neighbor search task based on cosine similarity. This task is then solved approximately, but with probabilistic guarantees through Multiprobe-LSH for cosine similarity. Essentially, every profile yields a block containing its top-K nearest neighbors, which is similar to applying Meta-blocking, Cardinality Node Pruning in particular, on a set of blocks. There are important differences, though, on the implementation details of the two methods.

DeepER offers two ways for vectorizing profiles. The unsupervised one tokenizes the value of every attribute a_i and represents a_i as the average embeddings vector of its tokens. The profile vector is then created by concatenating the attribute vectors. The supervised approach passes the emdedding vector of each attribute value token through a bidirectional LSTM, whose final output corresponds to the profile vector. Both approaches are combined with the pre-trained embeddings of GloVe and with hyperlane LSH, which is quite efficient in practice.

AutoBlock uses cross-polytype LSH, which is also quite fast, due to its theoretically optimal query time. Its profile vectors rely on fastText: first, all attribute values are tokenized and the embedding of each token is computed. The token vectors are then aggregated into attribute vectors through an attention-based mechanism based on a bidirectional-LSTM. This computes a weighted average of the token vectors, with weights determined through training. Next, multiple blocking keys are extracted from each profile using signature functions that combine attribute vectors. The blocking model is finally learned from training data so as to maximize the difference of the cosine similarities between the matching and non-matching profiles.

7.1.3   MATCHING

Most works on DL focus on Matching, modeling it as a binary classification problem. A large variety of techniques has been proposed in the last few years. We distinguish them into Generation 1 or 3, with the former including techniques for Transfer Learning, too. We delve into each category in the following.

Generation 1 Methods.   The following methods are schema-aware, operating on DSs with clean, aligned schemata. Therefore, they primarily target Veracity, aiming to maximize effectiveness despite the noise in attribute values.

DeepER [Ebraheem et al., 2018] adapts the approach described in Section 7.1.2 to Matching by creating a similarity vector for each pair of candidate matches, which is then fed to a binary classifier. The supervised approach subtracts (vector difference) or multiplies (hadamard product) the profile vectors of the candidate matches, while the unsupervised approach computes the cosine similarity for each pair of attribute vectors. Special care is taken to support the creation and tuning of local, i.e., learnable, embeddings, customized for the ER task at hand.

DeepMatcher [Mudgal et al., 2018] presents a framework for building DL-based Matching algorithms similar to the one outlined in Figure 7.1. Based on it, it proposes four models, all of which rely on pre-trained fastText embeddings. The two simplest ones resemble the two versions of DeepER, while the other two are more expressive and complex and, thus, more effective. One of them uses decomposable attention-based attribute summarization to create the attribute vector and concatenation for the pair vector. The last one, called hybrid, combines a bidirectional RNN with decomposable attention for the attribute vector and concatenation with element-wise absolute difference for the pair vector. These models are experimentally evaluated, showing their strengths and weaknesses.

Multi-Perspective Matching [Fu et al., 2019] adaptively selects the optimal similarity measures for three types of attributes: numeric, string, and textual (long strings). Several established measures are supported for each type of attributes, such as absolute difference for numbers, Jaro for strings, and two DeepMatcher architectures for texts. First, the comparison layer applies all similarity measures to every pair of attribute values. A gate mechanism selects the most appropriate similarity measure per attribute and the selected measures are concatenated into a comparison vector in the aggregation layer. Finally, a neural network receives the comparison vector as input and produces the matching probability as output.

CorDEL [Wang et al., 2020] goes beyond the above techniques, which rely on the twin-network architecture, by pre-processing the attribute values before building their vector representations. Given a pair of profiles, p_i and p_j, it tokenizes the value of every attribute to create three sets of words: one containing the words shared by p_i and p_j, one with the words appearing only in p_i, and one with the words appearing only in p_j. Every word in every set is vectorized with pre-trained fastText embeddings. A similarity vector is then created by aggregating the vectors for the first set of (common) tokens, while a difference vector is drawn from the other two sets of (unique) tokens. These two vectors are concatenated and forwarded to a classifier. *CorDEL-Sum* uses summation and MPLs for aggregation and classification, while attention mechanisms are used by *CorDEL-Attention* and *CorDEL-Context_Attention*.

Unlike the naive attention mechanisms of the above methods, the *Multi-Context Attention* framework [Zhang et al., 2020a] introduces a comprehensive mechanism that effectively captures the highly discriminative terms in a particular domain. Initially, it converts every attribute value into word embeddings with fastText. The resulting vectors are encoded by a BiGRU and self-attention to disambiguate and capture connections between the tokens. Then, pair-attention compares the tokens across the values of two profiles, jointly analyzing them while learning a similarity representation. The outputs of self- and pair-attention are fused through a highway network and the outcome is fed to a gating mechanism along with the original word vectors. The importance of contextual information is adjusted dynamically with appropriate weights. The end result is fed to a global attention module, which promotes the most discriminative terms. The representations learned for the two attribute values are then fused and given as input to a binary classifier.

Transfer Learning. DL models are data hungry, requiring thousands of labeled instances for training. Otherwise, their performance degrades significantly, even compared to traditional machine learning models [Kasai et al., 2019].

To address this shortcoming, the end-to-end framework *AutoEM* [Zhao and He, 2019] relies on the idea that most attributes in ER tasks over relational data belong to specific common types (e.g., person or product names). Hence, we can pre-train attribute-level classifiers on datasets with abundant labeled instances. For instance, a knowledge base like Wikipedia contains plenty of synonyms (i.e., positive instances) for person names, such as "Bill Gates" and "William Gates." Successfully applying these pre-trained models is a matter of correctly identifying the attribute types in the input DSs. In case a single attribute belongs to multiple types, the corresponding pre-trained type-specific models should be applied. If no known type is applicable, a pre-trained unified model is applied, which has been learned by using the union of the labeled instances of all known types. These models involve a complex hierarchy that combines character and word embeddings with BiGRU, while the final prediction is made by an MLP.

Finally, a holistic, table-level model is applied, trained over few labeled instances to learn the relative importance of attributes.

Transfer learning is combined with active learning (similar to LFP/LFN [Qian et al., 2017]) in Kasai et al. [2019] to further reduce the required number of labeled instances. In a nutshell, every attribute value is treated as a sequence of words, with every word vectorized through fastText. Every set of vectors is converted into an attribute representation through a BiGRU, and the similarity of two attributes is computed as the element-wise absolute difference of their vector representations. By adding the attribute similarities into a single vector, it estimates the similarity of every profile, which is then fed to an MLP for classification. This architecture is used for building a dataset classifier that predicts the source dataset of every profile pair. Adversarial transfer learning is used in this process, with part of the network trying to mislead the classifier so as to learn a robust, generic model.

Generation 3 Methods. The requirement for aligned schemata is waived by more recent techniques that leverage pre-trained transformer-based language models. These methods are able to target both Veracity and Variety, maximizing the effectiveness despite the heterogeneous attributes and the noise in their values.

The method presented in Teong et al. [2020] essentially concatenates all attribute values of a profile into a sentence. The sentences of a pair of candidate matches is then given as input to a BERT model, using special symbols to designate their beginning and to separate the two profiles. BERT is fine-tuned with a training set and its outcome is passed through a binary classifier for the match decision.

A very similar approach is examined in Brunner and Stockinger [2020], which considers more language models, like XLNet, RoBERTa, and DistilBERT. Among them, RoBERTa achieves the best performance.

This schema-agnostic approach can be successfully applied to models like Deep-Matcher [Li et al., 2020], too. However, it disregards valuable information about the entity structure and the boundaries of the attributes inside every profile. Better results are achieved by techniques that inherently support high levels of Variety.

To this end, *DITTO* [Li et al., 2020] uses RoBERTa, too, but includes the attribute names (with appropriate tags) in the sentence that represents every profile. It also introduces three optimizations. First, it incorporates domain knowledge by normalizing part of the attribute values (e.g., how many decimals in real numbers) as well as through a Named Entity Recognition model that identifies entity types and their properties (e.g., the address of an organization). Special tags are used to highlight this information. Second, it summarizes excessively large profiles by retaining the top non-stopword tokens according to a TF-IDF weighting scheme. The reason is that the language models receive up to 512 tokens as input. Third, it augments the training data with difficult examples, using a series of perturbation operators. Overall, the first two optimizations emphasize the most important information in the input profiles, while the last one allows for reducing the size of the training set.

Seq2SeqMatcher [Nie et al., 2019] reduces Matching to a token-level sequence-to-sequence matching problem. First, it converts every profile into a sequence of <attribute, word> pairs, where the attribute is represented by a custom, learned embedding, while the word embedding is derived from pre-trained fastText. Then, a bidirectional attention mechanism is applied to the sequences of two profiles and the k max attention scores create the soft-attended representation of each token. An aggregation layer gathers the resulting matching signals into two feature vectors, one for each entity, and forwards them to the prediction layer.

HierMatcher [Fu et al., 2020] builds a hierarchical network that performs matching at three levels: token, attribute and profile. First, it tokenizes every attribute value and vectorizes every token with pre-trained fastText embeddings. A BiGRU is then used to build an attribute representation. The next layer performs cross-attribute token alignment: given two profiles, p_i and p_j, it matches every attribute value token from p_i with the most similar one in p_j, regardless of the corresponding attributes. Next, the attribute layer aggregates the results of the previous layer through an attention mechanism that emphasizes the most important information per attribute. Finally, the entity layer concatenates the outcomes of the previous layer into a comparison vector that is fed to classification layer that produces a matching probability. All these components/layers of the neural network are learnable.

EmdDI [Cappuzzo et al., 2020] coins a graph-based approach for learning local embeddings, tailored to the ER task at hand. First, it converts the input relational databases into a tripartite graph, which includes three types of nodes: record (i.e., profile) ids, column (i.e., attribute) ids and tokens from all attribute values. The edges between the token nodes and the other two categories reflect the structural relationships in the schema of the input DSs. The similarity between these nodes is then captured through random walks, which are treated as sentences. These sentences are aggregated into a corpus that is then used for training embeddings with a common algorithm like word2vec, GloVe, or fastText.

On a different direction, Schneider et al. [2018] tackles ER by leveraging user-generated content that is publicly available on the Web. For each input profile, it aggregates all relevant user reviews (e.g., about a restaurant) into a user review document. Each word is vectorized through word2vec embeddings, while every document is represented as a binary or weighted bag-of-words vector. The duplicate entities are detected by applying the Word Mover's Distance to the document and word representations in combination with a clustering algorithm—stable marriage for Clean-Clean ER and Sequential Rippling for Dirty ER. Note that this approach can be combined with a traditional supervised Matching method, by treating its Word Mover's Distance as an additional feature.

Transfer Learning. It is worth stressing that all methods based on transformer-based language models perform transfer learning, too, in the sense that they use a labeled dataset to fine-tune pre-trained models.

Figure 7.2: In crowdsourced ER, the workers, i.e., humans, are asked about the relation between profiles for a small compensation per reply.

Discussion.   The DL-based methods, especially those of Generation 3, consistently achieve the best performance across a series of established benchmark datasets [Li et al., 2020]. Despite their high effectiveness, though, they suffer from very low time efficiency, requiring hours of training even over datasets with few thousand entities [Brunner and Stockinger, 2020]. No work so far examines ways of parallelizing or accelerating their training and application time. The only relevant efforts try to reduce the *complexity* of the learned models, which depends largely on the parameters that should be fine-tuned during training. Still, most DL models involve a sizable number of parameters: more than 22 million for the hybrid model of Deep-Matcher, around 700,000 for DeepMatcher-SIF and CorDel-Sum, and more than 500,000 for CorDel-Attention [Wang et al., 2020]. Special care should also be taken to build stable, robust and thus reliable models, such that different training runs yield insignificant variations in effectiveness [Wang et al., 2020].

7.2   CROWDSOURCED ENTITY RESOLUTION

Crowdsourcing examines mechanisms that push difficult tasks, called *Human Intelligence Tasks* (HITs), to humans, referred to as *workers* [Howe, 2006]. Typically, workers receive a small payment for each task they perform. The basic idea here is to crowdsource tasks that are complex for computers, but simple for humans. Due to its popularity, there are online communities that facilitate crowdsourcing, such as *Amazon Mechanical Turk*[2] and *Appen*[3] (previously known as Figure Eight and CrowdFlower).

In the case of ER, one of the most difficult tasks is to decide whether two profiles match or not, as shown in Figure 7.2. Crowdsourced ER assumes that humans can improve the effectiveness (i.e., accuracy) of Matching by leveraging contextual information and common sense. Therefore, it asks workers questions about the relation between profiles for a small compensation per reply.

[2]https://www.mturk.com
[3]https://appen.com

Four main challenges arise in this context [Christophides et al., 2020]:

- [Ch1] How should HITs be generated?

- [Ch2] How should HITs be formulated?

- [Ch3] How can we maximize accuracy, while minimizing the monetary cost?

- [Ch4] How can we restrict the development cost of Crowdsourced ER?

Below, we discuss the main solutions for addressing each challenge.

Methods for Challenge Ch1.   To generate HITs, a hybrid human–machine approach is invariably used [Chen, 2015, Li et al., 2017]. Initially, machine-based techniques perform a coarse pass over all pairs of candidate matches, discarding the majority of non-matches. This part typically involves a simple Generation 1 workflow that consists of Blocking and Matching. The workers are subsequently asked to verify the remaining profile pairs by generating one HIT per candidate match.

This two-step, hybrid approach was coined by *CrowdER* [Wang et al., 2012a], which automatically computes the similarity between profile pairs. Those below a predetermined threshold are discarded, while the ambiguous pairs are formulated as HITs. Although this approach is able to filter out a large number of pairs, it still has a significant overhead due to its cluster-based HITs (see Challenge Ch2, below).

A similar approach was introduced by *ZenCrowd* [Demartini et al., 2012]. Its machine-based pre-processing associates every profile with a ranking list of the most similar candidate matches using the TF-IDF similarity. To discard the obvious non-matches, it sets a threshold on the ranking function or on the number of retrieved profiles. During the crowdsourcing step, it dynamically assesses the quality of worker decisions using a probabilistic model. Each worker is assigned a prior probability based on a training set, but as more decisions are made, this probability is updated in order to detect unreliable workers. These workers are ignored by setting a threshold on the probability estimates for accepting a pair of profiles as a match.

Methods for Challenge Ch2.   The goal in addressing this challenge is to devise the best user interface for presenting HITs to workers.

The naive approach, called *pair-based HIT*, generates one HIT per pair of candidate matches, asking workers questions of the form "is p_i matching with p_j?" [Firmani et al., 2016, Verroios and Garcia-Molina, 2015, Vesdapunt et al., 2014, Wang et al., 2013, Whang et al., 2013a]. This results in simple, easy, and comprehensible tasks that allow workers to provide more accurate responses, as they focus on two specific profiles in every case. On the downside, this approach is not scalable, due to its quadratic complexity with respect to the temporal and monetary cost.

An alternative formulation involves *cluster-based* (or *multi-item*) *HITs*, which pertain to groups of $k > 2$ profiles, and every worker is requested to mark all duplicates within each

Figure 7.3: A simple illustration of HITs: cluster-based (left) and pair-based (right).

group [Wang et al., 2012a]. Figure 7.3 juxtaposes this kind of HITs (on the left) with the pair-based ones (on the right). A cluster-based HIT with many matches requires fewer comparisons than a pair-based HIT, enabling workers to mark many pairs of profiles with a few clicks. Assuming n profiles as input, the crowdsourced complexity is reduced to $O(n^2/k^2)$, but remains high, while the effectiveness is lower than the pair-based HITs, because the tasks are more complex and because two duplicate profiles are matched only if they co-occur in a HIT. Besides, generating cluster-based HITs is an NP-hard problem that is solved approximately by CrowdER through a greedy algorithm [Wang et al., 2012a].

Hybrid HITs are used by *Waldo* [Verroios et al., 2017]. The rationale is that workers are not infallible; in fact, their error rate is different for different profile pairs. Hence, the most "difficult" (i.e., high error-rate) pairs should be formulated as pair-based HITs, whereas the all other (i.e., low error-rate) pairs should form cluster-based HITs. Generating the best hybrid HITs within a given budget is an optimization task that is solved with probabilistic guarantees by Waldo.

Finally, *attribute-level HITs* are used in *Crowdlink* [Zhang et al., 2015]. The profile pairs with overwhelming information (i.e., complex structures and attributes) are decomposed into attribute-level HITs. A probabilistic framework then selects the k best attributes that satisfy the user requirements.

Methods for Challenge Ch3.   To optimize the trade-off between accuracy and monetary cost, the transitive relation is typically leveraged: if the relation between two profiles can be inferred by transitivity from the already detected duplicates, it is not crowdsourced. This inference takes two flavors [Chen, 2015]:

1. *positive transitivity* suggests that if $p_i \equiv p_j$ and $p_j \equiv p_k$, then $p_i \equiv p_k$; and

2. *negative transitivity* indicates that if $p_i \equiv p_j$, but $p_j \not\equiv p_k$, then $p_i \not\equiv p_k$.

These relations lie at the core of several approaches that minimize the number of HITs submitted to workers, reducing significantly the crowdsourcing overhead. Their key insight is that finding matches before non-matches accelerates the ER process, by making the most of the transitive closure. This is an NP-hard problem that is approximately solved with heuristics.

In more detail, *edge-centric ordering* [Wang et al., 2013] sorts and processes the profile pairs in decreasing matching likelihood. A similarity graph captures the cluster associated with every profile at the moment. If no match decision can be deduced from the similarity graph, the current pair is crowdsourced.

Node-centric ordering [Vesdapunt et al., 2014] sorts individual profiles in decreasing overall matching likelihood. Starting with the top profile p_i, its matching candidates are sorted and processed in decreasing overall matching likelihood; every pair is then crowdsourced until finding the first match for p_i.

Both algorithms are extended in Firmani et al. [2016] so that they iteratively crowdsource the profile pair that maximizes the expected marginal gain in recall.

Finally, a probabilistic framework for selecting the crowdsourced profile pairs is presented in Whang et al. [2013a]. It transforms the output of a similarity measure into a probability function and estimates the expected accuracy by crowdsourcing a particular pair in combination with transitive closure. Analytically computing the optimal pair order in this context is a #P-hard problem that is solved with heuristics.

However, the above methods assume that workers are infallible, operating as a perfect oracle, which means that uncertainty comes exclusively from the machine-generated similarities. In reality, though, even high-accuracy workers have an error rate up to 25% for various reasons, such as lack of domain expertise, task complexity or ambiguity, and tiredness [Wang et al., 2015]. When human errors occur, the above methods amplify them, which eventually compromises the overall accuracy [Wang et al., 2015]. A generic but naive solution would be to assign the same HIT to multiple workers and reconcile their responses through majority voting, but errors are still possible [Wang et al., 2015, Yalavarthi et al., 2017]. Hence, there is a need for specialized and robust approaches that inherently tackle **noisy workers**, minimizing HITs despite the uncertainty introduced by possibly false match decisions.

Adaptive Crowd-based Deduplication [Wang et al., 2015] reconciles inconsistent crowd results by increasing the monetary cost: the initial entities, produced by Correlation Clustering, are refined with additional HITs and a series of split and merge operations.

Attribute Labeling and Clustering [Khan and Garcia-Molina, 2016] mitigates errors by soliciting new metadata about the given profiles from the crowd (e.g., "label the attribute 'Type of celebrity' with 'Actor/Actress,' 'Singer' or 'Athlete'"). Using a probabilistic model, it optimizes the labeling process for a given recall.

The framework presented in Chai et al. [2016] relies on a partial-order of candidate matches, where a pair $< p_i, p_j >$ dominates another one $< p_k, p_l >$ if $< p_i, p_j >$ has no smaller similarities on every attribute than $< p_k, p_l >$. Partial order and transitivity is also used in Li [2017] for refining crowd disagreements.

bDENSE [Verroios and Garcia-Molina, 2015] models crowdsourced ER as a Maximum Likelihood Clustering of the similarity graph, an NP-hard problem that is approximately solved through a novel algorithm called Spectral-Connected-Components. A similar approach that selects the crowdsourced pairs based on global (rather than local) information is presented in Yalavarthi et al. [2017].

Finally, a flexible approach that can be combined with any method assuming infallible workers is the *Pair-wise Error Correction Layer* [Galhotra et al., 2018]. To add a profile to an entity, it requires a specific number of positive answers to random, "control queries." It also involves a merge phase that boosts recall and a split phase that boosts precision.

Methods for Challenge Ch4.   The above approaches have a rather limited scope, as they crowdsource part of the end-to-end ER workflow, usually Matching. They also involve a high developer cost, because their implementation is usually specific to a particular ER problem, i.e., they are difficult to generalize to other ER problems. Considering their monetary cost, too, it is no surprise that such task-specific implementations are restricted to ER tasks with large budgets.

To address these issues, *Corleone* [Gokhale et al., 2014] implements a hands-off approach for the entire ER workflow of Generation 1. Corleone is generic enough to support any application, involves no software developers (i.e., zero development cost) and is suitable even for lay users. It automatically generates blocking rules, learns a matcher from the HITs that are iteratively answered by workers and finally returns the detected entities. Active learning is leveraged to minimize the monetary cost, an approach that is also used in Mozafari et al. [2014].

However, Corleone runs in-memory on a single machine. As a result, it suffers from poor scalability and very low time efficiency, much lower than that of automatic solutions for Matching, due to the long latency of workers. To accelerate Crowdsourced ER, *Falcon* [Das et al., 2017] enhances Corleone's poor scalability by transforming the ER workflow into a set of operations that involve both machine and crowd activities. Their execution is optimized to minimize the overall running time, using massive parallelization on top of Apache Hadoop, while running as many machine activities as possible during crowdsourcing. Experiments show that it scales to 1–2.5 million profiles for just $60 in 2–14 hours.

However, Falcon is capable of handling a single ER process at a time. *Cloud-Matcher* [Govind et al., 2018] implements Falcon as a cloud service, extending it to handle multiple concurrent ER workflows.

CHAPTER 8

Resources for Entity Resolution

We now provide an overview of the available resources for developing, evaluating and comparing ER methods.

8.1 ER TOOLS

There is a plethora of ER systems that implement some of the aforementioned, established approaches or even custom ones. To present them in an organized way, we rely on the main requirements that have been specified in the literature. In more detail, ER systems should:

(R_1) be extensible, open-source tools [Golshan et al., 2017],

(R_2) cover the entire end-to-end pipeline [Konda et al., 2016],

(R_3) process data of any structuredness [Golshan et al., 2017],

(R_4) require no coding from their users [Konda et al., 2016],

(R_5) provide guidelines for creating effective solutions [Konda et al., 2016], and

(R_6) exploit a wide range of techniques [Konda et al., 2016].

Due to the first requirement (R_1), we focus exclusively on open-code systems, which additionally provide more information about their internal functionality.[1] Moreover, we require that every considered system satisfies the second requirement (R_2), implementing an end-to-end workflow of at least two-steps, i.e., Blocking and Matching, so that it combines high effectiveness with high time efficiency. The requirements R_3, R_4, and R_5 are examined in Table 8.1, which presents the main technical characteristics per ER tool—R_3 corresponds to second column ("Input Formats"), R_4 to the column "GUI" and R_5 to the rightmost column, "Help." Note that we do not report the supported output formats, as not all tools facilitate the storage of final or intermediate results; some tools merely present their results through their GUI, while others return custom data structures that require further processing by the user. Note also that we generalize requirement R_4 so as to exclude systems that involve heavy human intervention

---

[1]A detailed discussion about commercial (and some non-commercial systems) can be found in the extended version of Konda et al. [2016].

Table 8.1: Technical features of the main open-source ER systems. LB stands for Learning-based, NL for non-learning, C-C for Clean-Clean ER, and D for Dirty ER.

Tool	Input Formats	Learning	GUI	Language	Parallelization	Task	Help
Magellan	CSV	LB	Yes	Python	—	C-C	✓
DuDe	CSV, JSON, XML, BibTex, Database (Oracle, DB2, MySQL, and PostgreSQL)	NL	No	Java	—	C-C	—
FRIL	CSV, Excel, COL, Database	LB, NL	Yes	Java	—	D	—
OYSTER	Text-based	NL	No	Java	—	D	—
Record Linkage	Database	LB	No	R	—	C-C, D	—
CODI	RDF, OWL	NL	No	Java	—	C-C	—
LogMap	RDF, OWL	NL	Yes	Java	—	C-C	—

(a) Generation 1

Dedupe	CSV, SQL	LB	No	Python	multi-core	C-C, D	—
FAMER	JSON	NL	No	Java	Apache Flink	C-C	—
Febrl	CSV, text-based	LB, NL	Yes	Python	multi-core	C-C, D	—

(b) Generation 2

KnoFuss	RDF, SPARQL	LB	No	Java	—	C-C	—
SERIMI	SPARQL	NL	No	Ruby	—	C-C, D	—
Silk	RDF, SPARQL, CSV	LB	Yes	Scala	Apache Spark	D	✓
LIMES	RDF, SPARQL, CSV	LB	Yes	Java	multi-core	C-C	—
Winte.r	CSV, JSON, XML	LB	No	Java	—	C-C, D	—
Minoan-ER	RDF	NL	No	Java	Apache Spark	C-C, D	—

(c) Generation 3

JedAI	CSV, RDF/XML, RDF/HDT, RDF/JSON, OWL, Database (mySQL, PostgreSQL), SPARQL endpoint, Java serialized object	NL	Yes	Java	Apache Spark	C-C, D	✓

(d) Generation 4

from expert users, such as the recent crowdsourced systems Corleone [Gokhale et al., 2014] and Falcon [Das et al., 2017] as well as human-in-the-loop systems like SystemER [Qian et al., 2019]. The final requirement (R_6) is examined in Table 8.2, which reports the methods that are implemented by each ER tool for the two core workflow steps, i.e., Blocking and Matching. The latter involves not only similarity measures, but also filtering methods for accelerating the execution of matching rules. In both tables, the tools are grouped according to their generation.

We observe that Generations 1 and 2 include tools crafted exclusively for structured data: Magellan [Konda et al., 2016], Dedupe [Bilenko and Mooney, 2003], DuDe [Draisbach and Naumann, 2010], Febrl [Christen, 2008a], FRIL [Jurczyk et al., 2008], OYSTER [Talburt and Zhou, 2013], Record Linkage [Sariyar et al., 2011], and FAMER [Saeedi et al., 2018a]. Most of them merely apply the required two-step end-to-end workflow. For Blocking, each tool provides few custom or established methods, except for Febrl, which offers the schema-based implementation of the main local and global techniques. For Matching, each tool provides various similarity measures, with Magellan offering the main similarity join techniques, too. Note that Dedupe and FAMER are the only tools that apply Clustering. The former applies a simple hierarchical method to enhance its Matching, whereas the latter implements various established techniques, focusing on Multi-source ER. Note also that only Febrl and FRIL offer a GUI for ease of use. Finally, Dedupe, Febrl, and FAMER support parallelization for at least one workflow step, thus belonging to Generation 2.

Generation 3 primarily includes Link Discovery frameworks, which are crafted for semistructured data that are described by high quality ontologies. They implement a schema-based workflow that consists of Blocking and Matching, with some of them being able to apply it to structured data, as well. As a result, most of these tools are capable of tackling limited levels of Variety. The only exception is MinoanER [Efthymiou et al., 2019], which implements a schema-agnostic workflow that involves Block Processing, too. For Blocking, the tools of this generation generally offer custom approaches: KnoFuss [Nikolov et al., 2007] and SERIMI [Araújo et al., 2015] apply Token Blocking to the literal values of RDF triples, whereas Silk [Volz et al., 2009] implements MultiBlock [Isele et al., 2011], LIMES [Ngomo and Auer, 2011] its homonymous technique that relies on the triangle inequality in metric spaces and MinoanER Token Blocking along with Disjunctive Blocking on values and one-hop neighbors [Efthymiou et al., 2019]. Only Winte.r [Lehmberg et al., 2017] complements its custom methods with established ones, namely Standard Blocking and Sorted Neighborhood. All systems offer the main similarity measures, with LIMES further providing a set of established and custom similarity join techniques to accelerate their execution. Silk and LIMES are the only systems that provide a GUI and support parallelization. Parallelization is also an integral part of MinoanER. For a detailed overview of Link Discovery frameworks please see Nentwig et al. [2017b].

Generation 4 is represented only by JedAI [Papadakis et al., 2020a], which is capable of processing data of any structuredness both in a batch and in a progressive mode. JedAI implements a large variety of schema-based or schema-agnostic methods in each step of its budget-aware

Table 8.2: Methods per workflow step for the main open-source ER systems

Tool	Blocking	Entity Matching	
		Filtering	Similarity Measures
Magellan	SB, SN (also allows user-specified blocking patterns)	Overlap, Size, Prefix, Position, Suffix	Cosine, Dice, Edit distance, Jaccard, overlap, overlap coefficient
DuDe	SB, SN, Sorted blocks	—	BlockDistance, Cosine, Dice Coefficient, Euclidean Distance, Jaccard, Jaro Distance, Jaro-Winkler, Levenshtein, Matching Coefficient, Monge-Elkan, Needleman Wunsch, Overlap Coefficient, Smith-Waterman
FRIL	SB, SN	—	edit distance, Soundex, Q-gram, Equality(0-1)
OYSTER	SB	—	R-Swoosh
Record Linkage	SB (with SOUNDEX)	—	Uses statistics (ML) for different attributes' equivalence metrics to attain patterns-probabilities for false match rates
CODI	Logic-based constraints to exclude comparisons	—	threshold-based edit distance
LogMap	Logic-based constraints to exclude comparisons	—	ISUB [Stoilos et al., 2005]

(a) Generation 1

Tool	Blocking	Filtering	Similarity Measures
Dedupe	SB with learning-based techniques	—	Affine Gap Distance
FAMER	SB, SN, Q-Grams	—	Jaro-Winkler, TruncateBegin, TruncateEnd, edit distance, Monge-Elkan, Jaccard, Dice, Overlap Extended Jaccard, Longest Common Substring, Numerical Similarity Max Distance, Numerical Similarity Max Percentage
Febrl	SB, SN, Sorted blocks, **Suffix Arrays, Extended Q-Grams, Canopy Clustering, StringMap**	—	Bag-Dist, Dam-Le edit distance, edit distance, Editex, Jaro, Long-Common-Seq, Q-Gram, S-Gram, Smith-Waterman, Syll-Align-Dist, Winkler, string equality, Token-Set, TIME, Key-Dierence, Numeric

(b) Generation 2

Tool	Blocking	Filtering	Similarity Measures
KnoFuss	Literal Blocking	—	edit-distance (DATE, DiceCoefficient, Jaccard, Jaro, JaroWinkler, Overlap, Monge-Elkan, Smith-Waterman, Token Based, Token Wise)
SERIMI	Logic-based constraints to exclude comparisons	—	n-gram based
Silk	Multiblock	—	Jaro, Jaro-Winkler, QGram, string equality, numerical similarity, date, uri equality, taxonomic, max Set
LIMES	Custom methods	PPJoin+, Ed-Join, HR3, HYPPO, ORCHID	Cosine, ExactMatch, Jaccard, Jaro, Jaro-Winkler, Levenshtein, Monge-Elkan, Overlap, Q-Gram, Ratcli Obershelp, Soundex, Trigram
Winte.r	SB, SN, Custom methods	—	Jaccard, N-Grams, Levenshtein edit distance, Levenshtein, Maximum Of Token Containment, Numerical (absolute differences, deviation, unadjusted deviation, percentage), DATE (custom based, user specified)
Minoan-ER	SB	—	Value & Neighbor Similarity

(c) Generation 3

Tool	Blocking	Filtering	Similarity Measures
JedAI	SB, (Extended) SN, (Extended) Suffix Arrays, Min-Hash/Superbit LSH, (Extended) Q-Grams	AllPairs, PPJoin, FastSS, PassJoin, PartEnum, EdJoin, Silk-Moth	Group Linkage & Prole Matcher in combination with character & token n-gram graphs and containment, (normalized) value & overall graph similarity, or character & token n-grams and cosine, (generalized) Jaccard & SIGMA similarity, or pretrained embeddings and cosine similarity or Euclidean distance

(d) Generation 4

and budget-agnostic workflows. In any case, the selected pipeline can be executed either serially, on a single CPU, or in parallel, on top of Apache Spark. JedAI also applies seamlessly to both Clean-Clean and Dirty ER, unlike tools like Magellan and the Link Discovery frameworks, which are restricted to Clean-Clean ER. Regarding the ease of use, JedAI offers a *non-learning* functionality that can operate with default configurations, independently of a ground-truth—the ground-truth is only used for fine-tuning the parameters of its end-to-end pipelines and for benchmarking purposes. In contrast, the *learning-based* functionality of systems like Magellan, Silk, and LIMES requires a labeled dataset for its supervised operation; without such a dataset, they cannot define domain- and/or dataset-specific features and cannot learn any blocking or matching model.

8.2   ER DATASETS

Benchmark datasets are necessary for carrying out fundamental experimental evaluations, such as measuring the effectiveness and time efficiency of ER methods, determining their scalability and comparing their relative performance on an equal basis. Each dataset involves different characteristics and, thus, challenges. For example, one might contain few profiles described by structured data, while another might be a fairly large collection of semi-structured data. To provide a comprehensive evaluation of their approaches, researchers and practitioners typically perform the same evaluation over multiple datasets with different characteristics. Therefore, numerous, publicly available data sources are required for fostering the progress in ER.

Indeed, several benchmark datasets have been released over the years. To facilitate their use, we organize the main ones into a taxonomy that consists of the following six criteria.

1. *Origin*, which distinguishes benchmark datasets into real and synthetic ones. The former are static data collections that usually stem from existing applications and, thus, allow for testing ER methods in realistic settings. In contrast, the synthetic datasets are created artificially, usually from a small nucleus of real data, by simulating different forms of noise and errors (e.g., by adjusting the rate of missing values and/or typographical errors). Thus, their settings are less realistic, but more flexible, enabling researchers to focus on specific challenges. For example, they allow for assessing scalability simply by increasing their size.

2. *ER task*, which can be Clean-Clean ER (C-C), Dirty ER (D), or Multi-source ER (M). The last option is less frequent, as in practice, it can be simulated by putting together different instances of Clean-Clean or Dirty ER datasets.

3. *Generation*, which indicates the challenges conveyed by each dataset. Generation 1 corresponds to structured data of small or moderate size, Generation 2 to very large structured data, Generation 3 to semi-structured data of moderate or large size, and Generation 4 to streaming data of any structuredness.

4. *Golden standard*, which can be the complete ground-truth or a labeled dataset. The former comprises all positive instances, i.e., the existing pairs of matches, while the latter captures only a subset of these instances that suffices for training and testing a classification model. This subset is accompanied by a similar number of negative instances (non-matching profile pairs). The relative number and representativity of positive and negative instances affects significantly the performance of the learned model.

5. *Scope*, which indicates the workflow step(s) that can be evaluated by a dataset. Datasets of global scope can evaluate every workflow step, unlike the local scope datasets, which target a specific workflow step. Most often this step is Matching, as the dataset provides a specific set of candidate matches after Blocking.

The value of the main benchmark datasets for these criteria are listed in Table 8.3. For each dataset, its source is also reported, through a reference to the public repository that has released it. Note that some datasets appear in different forms. For example, an early version of Cora consists of ∼1,200 profiles, while the more recent one involves ∼1,800 profiles. In other cases, noise is added to a real dataset in order to stress and evaluate a specific characteristic. For example, dirty versions of DBLP-ACM, Walmart-Amazon, and others are produced in Mudgal et al. [2018] by switching the values of different attributes so as to raise the levels of schema heterogeneity (i.e., Variety). To facilitate reproducibility and to compare fairly the experiments across different works, the same version of datasets should be used together with the same preprocessing (if any).

As their name indicates, the datasets in Table 8.3 cover specific domains, including bibliographic (e.g., DBLP), product (e.g., Amazon), and census data (i.e., profiles about persons) or movies (e.g., IMDB). Some others are generic, including a wide range of domains, such as DBPedia. Note that most datasets pertain to Generation 1, while Generation 4 is represented by no dataset—typically, a static dataset is converted into a streaming one by making its profiles available one by one or in batches (e.g., in Karapiperis et al. [2018a]). For Generation 2, three datasets are frequently used, with each one comprising a series of synthetic datasets: Music Brainz involves three datasets with 20K, 2M, and 20M profiles, North Carolina Voters two datasets with 5M and 10M profiles, and Synthetic Census seven datasets with 5K, 10K, 50K, 100K, 200K, 300K, 1M, and 2M profiles. The Synthetic Census data have been generated by Febrl Christen [2008a] and are widely used in the literature for scalability analyses (e.g., in Kenig and Gal [2013], Papadakis et al. [2015, 2016b]).

For a more detailed discussion about real datasets, please refer to Primpeli and Bizer [2020]. Also worth noting is the *Ontology Alignment Evaluation Initiative*,[7] which every year organizes a contest that includes tasks for evaluating state-of-the-art ER systems over real and

---

[2]https://hpi.de/naumann/projects/repeatability/datasets.html
[3]https://dbs.uni-leipzig.de/research/projects/object_matching/benchmark_datasets_for_entity_resolution
[4]https://github.com/scify/JedAIToolkit/tree/master/data
[5]https://sites.google.com/site/anhaidgroup/useful-stuff/data
[6]http://webdatacommons.org/largescaleproductcorpus/v2/index.html
[7]http://oaei.ontologymatching.org

Table 8.3: The main benchmark datasets used for evaluating ER methods and systems. The source repositories are HPI,[2] UL,[3] JDI,[4] MGL,[5] and WDC.[6]

Name	Origin	Task	Gen.	Golden Standard	Scope	Source
CdDb	real	D	1	ground-truth	global	HPI
Census	real	D	1	ground-truth	global	HPI
Cora	real	D	1	ground-truth	global	HPI
Restaurants	real	D	1	ground-truth	global	HPI
DBLP-ACM	real	C-C	1	ground-truth	global	UL
DBLP-Scholar	real	C-C	1	ground-truth	global	UL
Amazon-GP	real	C-C	1	ground-truth	global	UL
Abt-Buy	real	C-C	1	ground-truth	global	UL
IMDB-DBPedia Movies	real	C-C	1	ground-truth	global	JDI
Walmart-Amazon	real	C-C	1	ground-truth	global	MGL
Beer Advocate-Rate Beer	real	C-C	1	labelled dataset	global/local	MGL
iTunes-Amazon Music	real	C-C	1	labelled dataset	global/local	MGL
Baby Products	real	C-C	1	labelled dataset	global/local	MGL
Bikedekho-Bikewale	real	C-C	1	labelled dataset	global/local	MGL
Amazon-Sephora	real	C-C	1	labelled dataset	global/local	MGL
Music Brainz	synthetic	M	2	ground-truth	global	UL
North Carolina Voters	synthetic	M	2	ground-truth	global	UL
Synthetic Census	synthetic	D	2	ground-truth	global	JDI
DBPedia 3.0rc-3.4	real	C-C	3	ground-truth	global	JDI
cameras	real	D	3	labelled dataset	global/local	WDC
watches	real	D	3	labelled dataset	global/local	WDC
computers	real	D	3	labelled dataset	global/local	WDC
shoes	real	D	3	labelled dataset	global/local	WDC

synthetic datasets. The results of every contest and track are published at a workshop that is typically collocated with the International Semantic Web conference.[8] Similar contests are sometimes organized by major data management conferences, e.g., the ACM SIGMOD Programming Contest 2020.[9]

Note also that for synthetic datasets, synthetic data generators can be used. These are systems like Febrl, SWING [Ferrara et al., 2011], LANCE [Saveta et al., 2015], and EMBench^{++}[Ioannou and Velegrakis, 2019] that allow researchers to control the modifications applied on the dataset as well as the level of each modification. For example, EMBench^{++} is based on a series of test cases that capture the majority of the ER situations. This includes modifications of the profiles (e.g., misspellings, abbreviations, acronyms), modifications over the relationships among profiles (e.g., additions, deletions) and data evolution. The latter allows for generating a series of datasets that are independent or every successive dataset is a modification of the previous one.

Finally, it is worth noting that there are generic datasets that are not originally created for ER. Yet, they can be used as ER benchmarks by leveraging their information. For example, the 2019 Billion Triple Challenge dataset [Herrera et al., 2019] as well as its earlier versions include `owl:sameAs` statements that indicate duplicate profiles; these statements can form a ground-truth after cleaning (e.g., after excluding entities that are comprised by more than 10 profiles [Papadakis et al., 2012]).

---

[8]http://swsa.semanticweb.org/content/international-semantic-web-conference-iswc
[9]http://www.inf.uniroma3.it/db/sigmod2020contest/index.html

CHAPTER 9

Possible Directions for Future Work

Although ER has been attracting the interest of several research groups for decades, there are still several open research problems and opportunities. The evolving nature of data and system challenges constitute the main challenges for possible work.

In Chapter 1, we mentioned that recent ER techniques have focused on handling the issues within a continuously increasing volume of input data, i.e., Velocity. Suggested solutions introduced new ER mechanisms, such as pay-as-you-go processing and query-driven resolution. So far, the proposed solutions have led to interesting results. However, this particular research area is still at its infancy, with a plethora of open research challenges. There are still various opportunities for developing techniques that provide ER-related services immediately, without any setup time or specialized indexing structures, where only the most frequent instance information is indexed. Exploring the possible improvements that can be made by using Deep Learning and Crowdsourcing techniques constitutes another intriguing field of research.

As discussed in Papadakis et al. [2020b], progressive ER methods can be of two types: schema-aware, requiring domain knowledge for performing the envisioned processing, or schema-agnostic, ignoring domain knowledge so as to handle more data-related challenges. For both types, though, more research is needed on dynamic methods that inherently address the noise of imperfect matching algorithms. A related research direction proposed in the literature (e.g., Vesdapunt et al. [2014]) is combining these methods with crowdsourcing mechanisms.

Dealing with very large data collections, i.e., Volume, is currently another prominent direction. A lot of research methods focus on this direction, and numerous mechanisms have been already suggested in Chapters 4 and 5. Yet, more solutions based on DL need to be investigated. Even though such methods achieve top performance in most ER workflow steps of Generation 1, their time efficiency is rather poor, due to their long training and testing times. The schema-agnostic nature of some approaches allow them to address Variety, at least to some extent, but more research is required for improving their scalability so that they can process voluminous data.

Another interesting aspect related to DL is *explainability*, which requires justifying the outcome of the ER techniques—not only for the matching decisions, but also for the non-matching ones. Explainability is especially important for crucial data such as those from the medical domain [Li et al., 2020]. For example, a recent methodology incorporates explainability into the learning process, yielding rules that are human-comprehensible [Qian et al., 2019]. Another methodology illustrated that explainability can be achieved by building ER techniques with interpretable ML models [Ebaid et al., 2019], such as LIME [Ribeiro et al., 2016], which can explain the predictions of any classifier by approximating it locally.

Evolution is another very interesting and intriguing data characteristic that researchers very recently started investigated. Despite the existence of related solutions (e.g., Papadakis et al. [2011a]), this area is still in its infancy with various open directions, as discussed in Section 6.2. Solutions in the above directions do not only require novel techniques, but also impose modifications and adaptations of the existing ER workflows. This is yet another open research direction, which primarily involves the automatic configuration of ER workflows.

We observe that in general, one or more parameters must be configured in practically every ER method. These configurations affect the efficiency and effectiveness of the methods to a significant extent. Improving the current situation requires further research. Investigate, for example, how to automatically configure the parameters of each method, as well as how to reconfigure them upon data or system modifications.

Dealing with algorithmic bias within ER methods is another interesting research direction. We note that the configuration of methods, the characteristics of particular data sources (e.g., data with hidden correlations), or the mechanisms employed for performing matching, might cause discrimination [Hajian et al., 2016]. This gives rise to new research opportunities. Examples include discovering the reasons for bias within existing ER mechanisms, as well as developing fairness-aware steps in the existing ER workflows.

Finally, challenging research directions also lie beyond the design of new ER methods. One such opportunity is developing tools for Generation 4; as shown in Tables 8.1 and 8.2, only JedAI belongs to this category at the moment. Another prominent research direction is generating resolution-related data for benchmarking ER systems. The goal here is to keep up with the evolving challenges of ER. Realistic data should reflect the challenges that selected ER techniques focus on, while also capturing the properties of the corresponding real-world data.

Bibliography

Noha Adly. Efficient record linkage using a double embedding scheme. In *DMIN*, pages 274–281, 2009. 23

Akiko N. Aizawa and Keizo Oyama. A fast linkage detection scheme for multi-source information integration. In *WIRI*, pages 30–39, 2005. DOI: 10.1109/wiri.2005.2 19

Yasser Altowim and Sharad Mehrotra. Parallel progressive approach to entity resolution using MapReduce. In *ICDE*, pages 909–920, 2017. DOI: 10.1109/icde.2017.139 90

Yasser Altowim, Dmitri V. Kalashnikov, and Sharad Mehrotra. Progressive approach to relational entity resolution. *PVLDB*, 7(11):999–1010, 2014. DOI: 10.14778/2732967.2732975 91

Hotham Altwaijry, Sharad Mehrotra, and Dmitri V. Kalashnikov. Query: A framework for integrating entity resolution with query processing. *PVLDB*, 9(3):120–131, 2015. DOI: 10.14778/2850583.2850587 83, 95

Hotham Altwaijry, Dmitri V. Kalashnikov, and Sharad Mehrotra. QDA: A query-driven approach to entity resolution. *TKDE*, 29(2):402–417, 2017. DOI: 10.1109/tkde.2016.2623607 83, 95

Arvind Arasu, Christopher Ré, and Dan Suciu. Large-scale deduplication with constraints using dedupalog. In *ICDE*, pages 952–963, 2009. DOI: 10.1109/icde.2009.43 37

Arvind Arasu, Michaela Götz, and Raghav Kaushik. On active learning of record matching packages. In *SIGMOD*, pages 783–794, 2010. DOI: 10.1145/1807167.1807252 31, 33, 34

Samur Araújo, Duc Thanh Tran, Arjen P. de Vries, and Daniel Schwabe. SERIMI: class-based matching for instance matching across heterogeneous datasets. *TKDE*, 27(5):1397–1410, 2015. DOI: 10.1109/tkde.2014.2365779 75, 113

Javed A. Aslam, Ekaterina Pelekhov, and Daniela Rus. The star clustering algorithm for static and dynamic information organization. *Journal of Graph Algorithms and Applications*, 8(1):95–129, 2004. DOI: 10.7155/jgaa.00084 46

Ali Assi, Hamid Mcheick, and Wajdi Dhifli. BIGMAT: A distributed affinity-preserving random walk strategy for instance matching on knowledge graphs. In *IEEE Big Data*, pages 1028–1033, 2019. DOI: 10.1109/bigdata47090.2019.9006348 73

Nikolaus Augsten and Michael H. Böhlen. *Similarity Joins in Relational Database Systems*. Morgan & Claypool Publishers, 2013. DOI: 10.2200/s00544ed1v01y201310dtm038 42, 43

Nikhil Bansal, Avrim Blum, and Shuchi Chawla. Correlation clustering. *Machine Learning*, 56(1–3):89–113, 2004. DOI: 10.1023/B:MACH.0000033116.57574.95 46

Nils Barlaug and Jon Atle Gulla. Neural networks for entity matching. *CoRR*, 2020. 98

Rohan Baxter, Peter Christen, Tim Churches, et al. A comparison of fast blocking methods for record linkage. In *KDD Workshops*, pages 25–27, 2003. 19

Roberto J. Bayardo, Yiming Ma, and Ramakrishnan Srikant. Scaling up all pairs similarity search. In *WWW*, pages 131–140, 2007. DOI: 10.1145/1242572.1242591 42, 43, 45

Zohra Bellahsene, Angela Bonifati, and Erhard Rahm, Eds. *Schema Matching and Mapping*, 1st ed., Springer, 2011. 49
DOI: 10.1145/1951365.1951431

Kedar Bellare, Suresh Iyengar, Aditya G. Parameswaran, and Vibhor Rastogi. Active sampling for entity matching with guarantees. *ACM Transactions on Knowl. Discov. Data*, 7(3):12:1–12:24, 2013. DOI: 10.1145/2513092.2500490 34

Omar Benjelloun, Hector Garcia-Molina, Heng Gong, Hideki Kawai, Tait Eliott Larson, David Menestrina, and Sutthipong Thavisomboon. D-Swoosh: A family of algorithms for generic, distributed entity resolution. In *ICDCS*, page 37, 2007. DOI: 10.1109/icdcs.2007.96 53

Omar Benjelloun, Hector Garcia-Molina, David Menestrina, Qi Su, Steven Euijong Whang, and Jennifer Widom. Swoosh: A generic approach to entity resolution. *VLDB J.*, 18(1):255–276, 2009. DOI: 10.1007/s00778-008-0098-x 40, 53

Philip A. Bernstein, Jayant Madhavan, and Erhard Rahm. Generic schema matching, ten years later. *PVLDB*, 4(11):695–701, 2011. DOI: 10.14778/3402707.3402710 15

Brenda Betancourt, Giacomo Zanella, Jeffrey W. Miller, Hanna M. Wallach, Abbas Zaidi, and Beka Steorts. Flexible models for microclustering with application to entity resolution. In *NIPS*, pages 1417–1425, 2016. 45

Alina Beygelzimer, Daniel J. Hsu, John Langford, and Tong Zhang. Agnostic active learning without constraints. In *NIIPS*, pages 199–207, 2010. 34

Indrajit Bhattacharya and Lise Getoor. A latent Dirichlet model for unsupervised entity resolution. In *SIAM*, pages 47–58, 2006. DOI: 10.1137/1.9781611972764.5 27, 38

Indrajit Bhattacharya and Lise Getoor. Collective entity resolution in relational data. *TKDD*, 1(1), 2007a. DOI: 10.1145/1217299.1217304 27, 36, 94

Indrajit Bhattacharya and Lise Getoor. Query-time entity resolution. *Journal of Artificial Intelligence Research*, 30:621–657, 2007b. DOI: 10.1613/jair.2290 83, 94

Guilherme Dal Bianco, Renata Galante, Marcos André Gonçalves, Sérgio D. Canuto, and Carlos Alberto Heuser. A practical and effective sampling selection strategy for large scale deduplication. *TKDE*, 27(9):2305–2319, 2015. DOI: 10.1109/tkde.2015.2416734 32

Guilherme Dal Bianco, Marcos André Gonçalves, and Denio Duarte. BLOSS: Effective meta-blocking with almost no effort. *Information Systems*, 75:75–89, 2018. DOI: 10.1016/j.is.2018.02.005 69

Mikhail Bilenko and Raymond J. Mooney. Adaptive duplicate detection using learnable string similarity measures. In *KDD*, pages 39–48, 2003. DOI: 10.1145/956750.956759 29, 113

Mikhail Bilenko, Raymond J. Mooney, William W. Cohen, Pradeep Ravikumar, and Stephen E. Fienberg. Adaptive name matching in information integration. *IEEE Intelligent Systems*, 18(5):16–23, 2003. DOI: 10.1109/mis.2003.1234765 25

Mikhail Bilenko, Sugato Basu, and Mehran Sahami. Adaptive product normalization: Using online learning for record linkage in comparison shopping. In *ICDM*, pages 58–65, 2005. DOI: 10.1109/icdm.2005.18 95

Mikhail Bilenko, Beena Kamath, and Raymond J. Mooney. Adaptive blocking: Learning to scale up record linkage. In *ICDM*, pages 87–96, 2006. DOI: 10.1109/icdm.2006.13 12, 21

Jens Bleiholder and Felix Naumann. Data fusion. *ACM Computing Surveys*, 41(1):2008. DOI: 10.1145/1456650.1456651 13

Christoph Böhm, Gerard de Melo, Felix Naumann, and Gerhard Weikum. LINDA: Distributed web-of-data-scale entity matching. In *CIKM*, pages 2104–2108, 2012. DOI: 10.1145/2396761.2398582 71, 80

Piotr Bojanowski, Edouard Grave, Armand Joulin, and Tomás Mikolov. Enriching word vectors with subword information. *Transactions of the Association of Computational Linguistics*, 5:135–146, 2017. DOI: 10.1162/tacl_a_00051 99

Panagiotis Bouros, Shen Ge, and Nikos Mamoulis. Spatio-textual similarity joins. *PVLDB*, 6(1):1–12, 2012. DOI: 10.14778/2428536.2428537 43, 45

Sergey Brin and Lawrence Page. The anatomy of a large-scale hypertextual Web search engine. *Computer Networks*, 30(1–7):107–117, 1998. DOI: 10.1016/s0169-7552(98)00110-x 35

Ursin Brunner and Kurt Stockinger. Entity matching with transformer architectures—A step forward in data integration. In *EDBT*, pages 463–473, 2020. DOI: 10.5441/002/edbt.2020.58 103, 105

Paul Suganthan G. C., Adel Ardalan, AnHai Doan, and Aditya Akella. Smurf: Self-service string matching using random forests. *PVLDB*, 12(3):278–291, 2018. DOI: 10.14778/3291264.3291272 40

Yunbo Cao, Zhiyuan Chen, Jiamin Zhu, Pei Yue, Chin-Yew Lin, and Yong Yu. Leveraging unlabeled data to scale blocking for record linkage. In *IJCAI*, pages 2211–2217, 2011. DOI: 10.5591/978-1-57735-516-8/IJCAI11-369 21

Riccardo Cappuzzo, Paolo Papotti, and Saravanan Thirumuruganathan. Creating embeddings of heterogeneous relational datasets for data integration tasks. In *SIGMOD*, pages 1335–1349, 2020. DOI: 10.1145/3318464.3389742 104

Chengliang Chai, Guoliang Li, Jian Li, Dong Deng, and Jianhua Feng. Cost-effective crowd-sourced entity resolution: A partial-order approach. In *SIGMOD*, pages 969–984, 2016. DOI: 10.1145/2882903.2915252 108

Moses Charikar, Chandra Chekuri, Tomás Feder, and Rajeev Motwani. Incremental clustering and dynamic information retrieval. *SIAM Journal on Computing*, 33(6):1417–1440, 2004. DOI: 10.1137/s0097539702418498 95

Surajit Chaudhuri, Venkatesh Ganti, and Rajeev Motwani. Robust identification of fuzzy duplicates. In *ICDE*, pages 865–876, 2005. DOI: 10.1109/icde.2005.125 26, 27, 35

Surajit Chaudhuri, Venkatesh Ganti, and Raghav Kaushik. A primitive operator for similarity joins in data cleaning. In *ICDE*, pages 5–5, 2006. DOI: 10.1109/icde.2006.9 43

Surajit Chaudhuri, Bee-Chung Chen, Venkatesh Ganti, and Raghav Kaushik. Example-driven design of efficient record matching queries. In *PVLDB*, pages 327–338, 2007. 27, 40

Xiao Chen. Crowdsourcing entity resolution: A short overview and open issues. In *GvD*, pages 72–77, 2015. 106, 107

Zhaoqi Chen, Dmitri V. Kalashnikov, and Sharad Mehrotra. Exploiting context analysis for combining multiple entity resolution systems. In *SIGMOD*, pages 207–218, 2009. DOI: 10.1145/1559845.1559869 27, 30

Zhaoqiang Chen, Qun Chen, Boyi Hou, Zhanhuai Li, and Guoliang Li. Towards interpretable and learnable risk analysis for entity resolution. In *SIGMOD*, pages 1165–1180, 2020. DOI: 10.1145/3318464.3380572 27, 30

Flavio Chierichetti, Nilesh N. Dalvi, and Ravi Kumar. Correlation clustering in MapReduce. In *KDD*, pages 641–650, 2014. DOI: 10.1145/2623330.2623743 54

Peter Christen. Febrl: An open source data cleaning, deduplication and record linkage system with a graphical user interface. In *KDD*, pages 1065–1068, 2008a. DOI: 10.1145/1401890.1402020 30, 113, 116

Peter Christen. Automatic record linkage using seeded nearest neighbour and support vector machine classification. In *KDD*, pages 151–159, 2008b. DOI: 10.1145/1401890.1401913 35

Peter Christen. *Data Matching—Concepts and Techniques for Record Linkage, Entity Resolution, and Duplicate Detection*. Springer, 2012a. DOI: 10.1007/978-3-642-31164-2 1, 3, 8, 15, 24, 38, 39

Peter Christen. A survey of indexing techniques for scalable record linkage and deduplication. *TKDE*, 24(9):1537–1555, 2012b. DOI: 10.1109/tkde.2011.127 3, 11, 12, 15, 17, 19, 21, 22, 23, 24, 68

Peter Christen, Ross W. Gayler, and David Hawking. Similarity-aware indexing for real-time entity resolution. In *CIKM*, pages 1565–1568, 2009. DOI: 10.1145/1645953.1646173 83, 92

Peter Christen, Dinusha Vatsalan, and Qing Wang. Efficient entity resolution with adaptive and interactive training data selection. In *ICDM*, pages 727–732, 2015. DOI: 10.1109/icdm.2015.63 32

Vassilis Christophides, Vasilis Efthymiou, and Kostas Stefanidis. *Entity Resolution in the Web of Data*. Morgan & Claypool Publishers, 2015. DOI: 10.2200/s00655ed1v01y201507wbe013 3, 5, 63, 64, 77

Vassilis Christophides, Vasilis Efthymiou, Themis Palpanas, George Papadakis, and Kostas Stefanidis. End-to-end entity resolution for big data: A survey. *ACM Computing Surveys*, 53(6):1–42, 2020. 3, 106

Xu Chu, Ihab F. Ilyas, and Paraschos Koutris. Distributed data deduplication. *PVLDB*, 9(11):864–875, 2016. DOI: 10.14778/2983200.2983203 52

Aaron Clauset, Mark E. J. Newman, and Cristopher Moore. Finding community structure in very large networks. *Physical Review E*, 70(6):066111, 2004. DOI: 10.1103/physreve.70.066111 69

Munir Cochinwala, Verghese Kurien, Gail Lalk, and Dennis E. Shasha. Efficient data reconciliation. *Information Sciences*, 137(1-4):1–15, 2001. DOI: 10.1016/s0020-0255(00)00070-0 27, 29

William W. Cohen. Data integration using similarity joins and a word-based information representation language. *ACM Transactions on Information Systems*, 18(3), 2000. DOI: 10.1145/352595.352598 25

William W. Cohen and Jacob Richman. Learning to match and cluster large high-dimensional data sets for data integration. In *KDD*, pages 475–480, 2002. DOI: 10.1145/775047.775116 27, 29

William W. Cohen, Pradeep Ravikumar, and Stephen E. Fienberg. A comparison of string distance metrics for name-matching tasks. In *IIWeb*, pages 73–78, 2003. 26

Isabel F. Cruz, Flavio Palandri Antonelli, and Cosmin Stroe. AgreementMaker: Efficient matching for large real-world schemas and ontologies. *PVLDB*, 2(2):1586–1589, 2009. DOI: 10.14778/1687553.1687598 58

Aron Culotta and Andrew McCallum. Joint deduplication of multiple record types in relational data. In *CIKM*, pages 257–258, 2005. DOI: 10.1145/1099554.1099615 27, 38

B. T. Dai, N. Koudas, D. Srivastava, A. K. H. Tung, and S. Venkatasubramanian. Validating multi-column schema matchings by type. In *ICDE*, pages 120–129, 2008. DOI: 10.1109/icde.2008.4497420 58

Nilesh N. Dalvi, Vibhor Rastogi, Anirban Dasgupta, Anish Das Sarma, and Tamás Sarlós. Optimal hashing schemes for entity matching. In *WWW*, pages 295–306, 2013. DOI: 10.1145/2488388.2488415 24

Sanjib Das, Paul Suganthan G. C., AnHai Doan, Jeffrey F. Naughton, Ganesh Krishnan, Rohit Deep, Esteban Arcaute, Vijay Raghavendra, and Youngchoon Park. Falcon: Scaling up hands-off crowdsourced entity matching to build cloud services. In *SIGMOD*, pages 1431–1446, 2017. DOI: 10.1145/3035918.3035960 109, 113

Moisés G. de Carvalho, Alberto H. F. Laender, Marcos André Gonçalves, and Altigran Soares da Silva. A genetic programming approach to record deduplication. *TKDE*, 24(3):399–412, 2012. DOI: 10.1109/tkde.2010.234 27, 30

Timothy de Vries, Hui Ke, Sanjay Chawla, and Peter Christen. Robust record linkage blocking using suffix arrays. In *CIKM*, pages 305–314, 2009. DOI: 10.1145/1645953.1645994 12, 24

Jeffrey Dean and Sanjay Ghemawat. MapReduce: Simplified data processing on large clusters. *Communications of the ACM*, 51(1):107–113, 2008. DOI: 10.1145/1327452.1327492 49

Gianluca Demartini, Djellel Eddine Difallah, and Philippe Cudré-Mauroux. ZenCrowd: Leveraging probabilistic reasoning and crowdsourcing techniques for large-scale entity linking. In *WWW*, pages 469–478, 2012. DOI: 10.1145/2187836.2187900 106

Dong Deng, Guoliang Li, He Wen, and Jianhua Feng. An efficient partition based method for exact set similarity joins. *PVLDB*, 9(4):360–371, 2015. DOI: 10.14778/2856318.2856330 53

Jacob Devlin, Ming-Wei Chang, Kenton Lee, and Kristina Toutanova. BERT: Pre-training of deep bidirectional transformers for language understanding. In *NAACL-HLT*, pages 4171–4186, 2019. 99

Debabrata Dey, Sumit Sarkar, and Prabuddha De. Entity matching in heterogeneous databases: A distance based decision model. In *HICSS*, pages 305–313, 1998. DOI: 10.1109/hicss.1998.649225 26, 27

Juan A. Díaz and Elena Fernández. A tabu search heuristic for the generalized assignment problem. *European Journal of Operational Research*, 132(1):22–38, 2001. DOI: 10.1016/s0377-2217(00)00108-9 45

Hong Hai Do and Erhard Rahm. COMA—A system for flexible combination of schema matching approaches. In *VLDB*, pages 610–621, 2002. DOI: 10.1016/b978-155860869-6/50060-3 16

AnHai Doan, Pedro M. Domingos, and Alon Y. Halevy. Reconciling schemas of disparate data sources: A machine-learning approach. In *SIGMOD*, pages 509–520, 2001. DOI: 10.1145/375663.375731 17

AnHai Doan, Jayant Madhavan, Pedro M. Domingos, and Alon Y. Halevy. Learning to map between ontologies on the semantic web. In *WWW*, pages 662–673, 2002. DOI: 10.1145/511446.511532 16, 17

Xin Dong, Alon Y. Halevy, and Jayant Madhavan. Reference reconciliation in complex information spaces. In *SIGMOD*, pages 85–96, 2005. DOI: 10.1145/1066157.1066168 36, 91

Xin Luna Dong and Felix Naumann. Data fusion—Resolving data conflicts for integration. *PVLDB*, 2(2):1654–1655, 2009. DOI: 10.14778/1687553.1687620 13

Xin Luna Dong and Theodoros Rekatsinas. Data integration and machine learning: A natural synergy. In *SIGMOD*, pages 1645–1650, 2018. DOI: 10.1145/3183713.3197387 31

Xin Luna Dong and Divesh Srivastava. *Big Data Integration*. Morgan & Claypool Publishers, 2015. DOI: 10.2200/s00578ed1v01y201404dtm040 3, 11, 12

Uwe Draisbach and Felix Naumann. Dude: The duplicate detection toolkit. In *QDB*, 2010. 113

Uwe Draisbach and Felix Naumann. A generalization of blocking and windowing algorithms for duplicate detection. In *ICDKE*, pages 18–24, 2011. DOI: 10.1109/icdke.2011.6053920 23, 24

Uwe Draisbach, Felix Naumann, Sascha Szott, and Oliver Wonneberg. Adaptive windows for duplicate detection. In *ICDE*, pages 1073–1083, 2012. DOI: 10.1109/icde.2012.20 22

Uwe Draisbach, Peter Christen, and Felix Naumann. Transforming pairwise duplicates to entity clusters for high-quality duplicate detection. *ACM Journal of Data and Information Quality*, 12(1):3:1–3:30, 2020. DOI: 10.1145/3352591 46, 48

Songyun Duan, Achille Fokoue, Oktie Hassanzadeh, Anastasios Kementsietsidis, Kavitha Srinivas, and Michael J. Ward. Instance-based matching of large ontologies using locality-sensitive hashing. In *ISWC*, pages 49–64, 2012. DOI: 10.1007/978-3-642-35176-1_4 58, 59

Amr Ebaid, Saravanan Thirumuruganathan, Walid G. Aref, Ahmed K. Elmagarmid, and Mourad Ouzzani. EXPLAINER: Entity resolution explanations. In *ICDE*, pages 2000–2003, 2019. DOI: 10.1109/icde.2019.00224 120

Muhammad Ebraheem, Saravanan Thirumuruganathan, Shafiq R. Joty, Mourad Ouzzani, and Nan Tang. Distributed representations of tuples for entity resolution. *PVLDB*, 11(11):1454–1467, 2018. DOI: 10.14778/3236187.3236198 100, 101

Vasilis Efthymiou, George Papadakis, George Papastefanatos, Kostas Stefanidis, and Themis Palpanas. Parallel meta-blocking: Realizing scalable entity resolution over large, heterogeneous data. In *IEEE Big Data*, pages 411–420, 2015a. DOI: 10.1109/bigdata.2015.7363782 78

Vasilis Efthymiou, Kostas Stefanidis, and Vassilis Christophides. Big data entity resolution: From highly to somehow similar entity descriptions in the Web. In *IEEE Big Data*, pages 401–410, 2015b. DOI: 10.1109/bigdata.2015.7363781 63, 64, 77

Vasilis Efthymiou, Kostas Stefanidis, and Vassilis Christophides. Minoan ER: Progressive entity resolution in the Web of data. In *EDBT*, pages 670–671, 2016. 73

Vasilis Efthymiou, George Papadakis, George Papastefanatos, Kostas Stefanidis, and Themis Palpanas. Parallel meta-blocking for scaling entity resolution over big heterogeneous data. *Information Systems*, 65:137–157, 2017. DOI: 10.1016/j.is.2016.12.001 78, 80

Vasilis Efthymiou, George Papadakis, Kostas Stefanidis, and Vassilis Christophides. Simplifying entity resolution on web data with schema-agnostic, non-iterative matching. In *ICDE*, pages 1296–1299, 2018. DOI: 10.1109/icde.2018.00134 73

Vasilis Efthymiou, George Papadakis, Kostas Stefanidis, and Vassilis Christophides. MinoanER: Schema-agnostic, non-iterative, massively parallel resolution of web entities. In *EDBT*, pages 373–384, 2019. 2, 68, 69, 73, 80, 113

Marc Ehrig, Steffen Staab, and York Sure. Bootstrapping ontology alignment methods with APFEL. In *ISWC*, pages 186–200, 2005. DOI: 10.1007/11574620_16 17

Mohamed G. Elfeky, Ahmed K. Elmagarmid, and Vassilios S. Verykios. TAILOR: A record linkage tool box. In *ICDE*, pages 17–28, 2002. DOI: 10.1109/icde.2002.994694 27, 30, 35

Ahmed K. Elmagarmid, Panagiotis G. Ipeirotis, and Vassilios S. Verykios. Duplicate record detection: A survey. *TKDE*, 19(1):1–16, 2007. DOI: 10.1109/tkde.2007.250581 3, 15, 39

Ahmed K. Elmagarmid, Ihab F. Ilyas, Mourad Ouzzani, Jorge-Arnulfo Quiané-Ruiz, Nan Tang, and Si Yin. NADEEF/ER: Generic and interactive entity resolution. In *SIGMOD*, pages 1071–1074, ACM, 2014. DOI: 10.1145/2588555.2594511 27, 39

Jérôme Euzenat and Pavel Shvaiko. *Ontology Matching*, 2nd ed., Springer, 2013. DOI: 10.1007/978-3-642-38721-0 58

Luiz Osvaldo Evangelista, Eli Cortez, Altigran Soares da Silva, and Wagner Meira Jr. Adaptive and flexible blocking for record linkage tasks. *JIDM*, 1(2):167–182, 2010. 21

Wenfei Fan, Xibei Jia, Jianzhong Li, and Shuai Ma. Reasoning about record matching rules. *PVLDB*, 2(1):407–418, 2009. DOI: 10.14778/1687627.1687674 27, 42

Ivan P. Fellegi and Alan B. Sunter. A theory for record linkage. *Journal of the American Statistical Association*, 64(328):1183–1210, 1969. DOI: 10.1080/01621459.1969.10501049 15, 19, 27, 28

Raul Castro Fernandez, Essam Mansour, Abdulhakim Ali Qahtan, Ahmed K. Elmagarmid, Ihab F. Ilyas, Samuel Madden, Mourad Ouzzani, Michael Stonebraker, and Nan Tang. Seeping semantics: Linking datasets using word embeddings for data discovery. In *ICDE*, pages 989–1000, 2018. DOI: 10.1109/icde.2018.00093 100

Alfio Ferrara, Stefano Montanelli, Jan Noessner, and Heiner Stuckenschmidt. Benchmarking matching applications on the semantic web. In *ESWC*, 2011. DOI: 10.1007/978-3-642-21064-8_8 118

Fabian Fier, Nikolaus Augsten, Panagiotis Bouros, Ulf Leser, and Johann-Christoph Freytag. Set similarity joins on MapReduce: An experimental survey. *PVLDB*, 11(10):1110–1122, 2018. DOI: 10.14778/3231751.3231760 53

Donatella Firmani, Barna Saha, and Divesh Srivastava. Online entity resolution using an oracle. *PVLDB*, 9(5):384–395, 2016. DOI: 10.14778/2876473.2876474 106, 108

Jeffrey Fisher, Peter Christen, Qing Wang, and Erhard Rahm. A clustering-based framework to control block sizes for entity resolution. In *KDD*, pages 279–288, 2015. DOI: 10.1145/2783258.2783396 65

Gary William Flake, Robert Endre Tarjan, and Kostas Tsioutsiouliklis. Graph clustering and minimum cut trees. *Internet Mathematics*, 1(4):385–408, 2003. DOI: 10.1080/15427951.2004.10129093 46

Michael J. Franklin, Alon Y. Halevy, and David Maier. From databases to dataspaces: A new abstraction for information management. *SIGMOD Record*, 34(4):27–33, 2005. DOI: 10.1145/1107499.1107502 92

Cheng Fu, Xianpei Han, Le Sun, Bo Chen, Wei Zhang, Suhui Wu, and Hao Kong. End-to-end multi-perspective matching for entity resolution. In *IJCAI*, pages 4961–4967, 2019. DOI: 10.24963/ijcai.2019/689 101

Cheng Fu, Xianpei Han, Jiaming He, and Le Sun. Hierarchical matching network for heterogeneous entity resolution. In *IJCAI*, pages 3665–3671, 2020. DOI: 10.24963/ijcai.2020/507 104

Ariel Fuxman, Mauricio A. Hernández, C. T. Howard Ho, Renée J. Miller, Paolo Papotti, and Lucian Popa. Nested mappings: Schema mapping reloaded. In *VLDB*, pages 67–78, 2006. 16

Sainyam Galhotra, Donatella Firmani, Barna Saha, and Divesh Srivastava. Robust entity resolution using random graphs. In *SIGMOD*, pages 3–18, 2018. DOI: 10.1145/3183713.3183755 109

Sainyam Galhotra, Donatella Firmani, Barna Saha, and Divesh Srivastava. Efficient and effective ER with progressive blocking. *CoRR*, 2020. 91

Leonardo Gazzarri and Melanie Herschel. Boosting blocking performance in entity resolution pipelines: Comparison cleaning using bloom filters. In *EDBT*, pages 419–422, 2020. DOI: 10.5441/002/edbt.2020.47 66, 70

Kleanthi Georgala, Daniel Obraczka, and Axel-Cyrille Ngonga Ngomo. Dynamic planning for link discovery. In *ESWC*, pages 240–255, 2018. DOI: 10.1007/978-3-319-93417-4_16 76

Lise Getoor and Ashwin Machanavajjhala. Entity resolution: Theory, practice and open challenges. *PVLDB*, 5(12):2018–2019, 2012. DOI: 10.14778/2367502.2367564 3, 30

Phan Giang. A machine learning approach to create blocking criteria for record linkage. *Health Care Management Science*, 18(1):93–105, 2015. DOI: 10.1007/s10729-014-9276-0 23, 74

Chaitanya Gokhale, Sanjib Das, AnHai Doan, Jeffrey F. Naughton, Narasimhan Rampalli, Jude W. Shavlik, and Xiaojin Zhu. Corleone: Hands-off crowdsourcing for entity matching. In *SIGMOD*, pages 601–612, 2014. DOI: 10.1145/2588555.2588576 109, 113

Behzad Golshan, Alon Y. Halevy, George A. Mihaila, and Wang-Chiew Tan.   Data integration: After the teenage years.   In *ACM PODS*, pages 101–106, 2017. DOI: 10.1145/3034786.3056124 57, 83, 111

Ian J. Goodfellow, Yoshua Bengio, and Aaron C. Courville. *Deep Learning*. MIT Press, 2016. DOI: 10.1007/978-3-642-36657-4_1 97, 98

Yash Govind, Erik Paulson, Palaniappan Nagarajan, Paul Suganthan G. C., AnHai Doan, Youngchoon Park, Glenn Fung, Devin Conathan, Marshall Carter, and Mingju Sun. Cloud-matcher: A hands-off cloud/crowd service for entity matching. *PVLDB*, 11(12):2042–2045, 2018. DOI: 10.14778/3229863.3236255 109

Luis Gravano, Panagiotis G. Ipeirotis, H. V. Jagadish, Nick Koudas, S. Muthukrishnan, and Divesh Srivastava. Approximate string joins in a database (almost) for free. In *VLDB*, pages 491–500, 2001. 43

Anja Gruenheid, Xin Luna Dong, and Divesh Srivastava. Incremental record linkage. *PVLDB*, 7(9):697–708, 2014. DOI: 10.14778/2732939.2732943 83, 95

Sudipto Guha, Nick Koudas, Amit Marathe, and Divesh Srivastava.   Merging the results of approximate match operations. In *VLDB*, pages 636–647, 2004. DOI: 10.1016/b978-012088469-8.50057-7 26

Sara Hajian, Francesco Bonchi, and Carlos Castillo.   Algorithmic bias: From discrimination discovery to fairness-aware data mining.   In *KDD*, pages 2125–2126, 2016. DOI: 10.1145/2939672.2945386 120

Alon Y. Halevy, Flip Korn, Natalya Fridman Noy, Christopher Olston, Neoklis Polyzotis, Sudip Roy, and Steven Euijong Whang.   Managing Google's data lake: An overview of the goods system. *IEEE Data Eng. Bull.*, 39(3):5–14, 2016. 83

David J. Hand and Peter Christen. A note on using the F-measure for evaluating record linkage algorithms. *Statistics and Computing*, 28(3):539–547, 2018. DOI: 10.1007/s11222-017-9746-6 11

Oktie Hassanzadeh and Renée J. Miller. Creating probabilistic databases from duplicated data. *VLDB Journal*, 18(5):1141–1166, 2009. DOI: 10.1007/s00778-009-0161-2 46

Oktie Hassanzadeh, Fei Chiang, Renée J. Miller, and Hyun Chul Lee. Framework for evaluating clustering algorithms in duplicate detection. *PVLDB*, 2(1):1282–1293, 2009. DOI: 10.14778/1687627.1687771 45, 46

Oktie Hassanzadeh, Ken Q. Pu, Soheil Hassas Yeganeh, Renée J. Miller, Lucian Popa, Mauricio A. Hernández, and Howard Ho.   Discovering linkage points over web data. *PVLDB*, 6(6):444–456, 2013. DOI: 10.14778/2536336.2536345 57, 59

Taher H. Haveliwala, Aristides Gionis, and Piotr Indyk. Scalable techniques for clustering the Web. In *WebDB*, pages 129–134, 2000. 46

Daniel Ayala Hernández, Inma Hernández, David Ruiz, and Erhard Rahm. LEAPME: Learning-based property matching with embeddings. *CoRR*, 2020. 100

Mauricio A. Hernández and Salvatore J. Stolfo. The merge/purge problem for large databases. In *SIGMOD*, pages 127–138, 1995. DOI: 10.1145/223784.223807 21, 89

Mauricio A. Hernández, Renée J. Miller, and Laura M. Haas. Clio: A semi-automatic tool for schema mapping. In *SIGMOD*, page 607, 2001. DOI: 10.1145/376284.375767 17

Mauricio A. Hernández, Georgia Koutrika, Rajasekar Krishnamurthy, Lucian Popa, and Ryan Wisnesky. HIL: A high-level scripting language for entity integration. In *EDBT*, pages 549–560, 2013. DOI: 10.1145/2452376.2452440 27, 39

José-Miguel Herrera, Aidan Hogan, and Tobias Käfer. BTC-2019: The 2019 billion triple challenge dataset. In *ISWC*, pages 163–180, 2019. DOI: 10.1007/978-3-030-30796-7_11 118

Boyi Hou, Qun Chen, Jiquan Shen, Xin Liu, Ping Zhong, Yanyan Wang, Zhaoqiang Chen, and Zhanhuai Li. Gradual machine learning for entity resolution. In *WWW*, pages 3526–3530, 2019. DOI: 10.1145/3308558.3314121 27, 35

Jeff Howe. The rise of crowdsourcing. *Wired Magazine*, 14(6):1–4, 2006. 105

Wei Hu, Jianfeng Chen, and Yuzhong Qu. A self-training approach for resolving object coreference on the semantic web. In *WWW*, pages 87–96, 2011. DOI: 10.1145/1963405.1963421 74

Ihab F. Ilyas and Xu Chu. Data cleaning. *ACM*, 2019. DOI: 10.1145/3310205 13

Ekaterini Ioannou and Yannis Velegrakis. Embench^{++}: Data for a thorough benchmarking of matching-related methods. *Semantic Web*, 10(2):435–450, 2019. DOI: 10.3233/SW-180331 118

Ekaterini Ioannou, Wolfgang Nejdl, Claudia Niederée, and Yannis Velegrakis. On-the-fly entity-aware query processing in the presence of linkage. *PVLDB*, 3(1):429–438, 2010. DOI: 10.14778/1920841.1920898 95

Robert Isele and Christian Bizer. Learning expressive linkage rules using genetic programming. *PVLDB*, 5(11):1638–1649, 2012. DOI: 10.14778/2350229.2350276 73

Robert Isele, Anja Jentzsch, and Christian Bizer. Efficient multidimensional blocking for link discovery without losing recall. In *WebDB*, 2011. 113

Matthew A. Jaro. Advances in record-linkage methodology as applied to matching the 1985 census of Tampa, Florida. *Journal of the American Statistical Association*, 84(406):414–420, 1989. DOI: 10.1080/01621459.1989.10478785 27, 28

Yu Jiang, Guoliang Li, Jianhua Feng, and Wen-Syan Li. String similarity joins: An experimental evaluation. *PVLDB*, 7(8):625–636, 2014. DOI: 10.14778/2732296.2732299 42, 43, 45

Liang Jin, Chen Li, and Sharad Mehrotra. Efficient record linkage in large data sets. In *DAS-FAA*, pages 137–146, 2003. DOI: 10.1109/dasfaa.2003.1192377 23

Pawel Jurczyk, James J. Lu, Li Xiong, Janet D. Cragan, and Adolfo Correa. Fine-grained record integration and linkage tool. *Birth Defects Research Part A: Clinical and Molecular Teratology*, 82(11):822–829, 2008. DOI: 10.1002/bdra.20521 113

Anna Jurek, Jun Hong, Yuan Chi, and Weiru Liu. A novel ensemble learning approach to unsupervised record linkage. *Information Systems*, 71:40–54, 2017. DOI: 10.1016/j.is.2017.06.006 35

Dmitri V. Kalashnikov and Sharad Mehrotra. Domain-independent data cleaning via analysis of entity-relationship graph. *ACM Transactions on Database Systems*, 31(2):716–767, 2006. DOI: 10.1145/1138394.1138401 36

Jaewoo Kang and Jeffrey F. Naughton. On schema matching with opaque column names and data values. In *SIGMOD*, pages 205–216, 2003. DOI: 10.1145/872757.872783 58

Dimitrios Karapiperis and Vassilios S. Verykios. A fast and efficient hamming LSH-based scheme for accurate linkage. *Knowledge and Information Systems*, 49(3):861–884, 2016. DOI: 10.1007/s10115-016-0919-y 23

Dimitrios Karapiperis, Dinusha Vatsalan, Vassilios S. Verykios, and Peter Christen. Efficient record linkage using a compact hamming space. In *EDBT*, pages 209–220, 2016. DOI: 10.5441/002/edbt.2016.21 23

Dimitrios Karapiperis, Aris Gkoulalas-Divanis, and Vassilios S. Verykios. Summarization algorithms for record linkage. In *EDBT*, pages 73–84, 2018a. DOI: 10.5441/002/edbt.2018.08 83, 93, 116

Dimitrios Karapiperis, Aris Gkoulalas-Divanis, and Vassilios S. Verykios. Fast schemes for online record linkage. *Data Mining and Knowledge Discovery*, 32(5):1229–1250, 2018b. DOI: 10.1007/s10618-018-0563-0 93

Jungo Kasai, Kun Qian, Sairam Gurajada, Yunyao Li, and Lucian Popa. Low-resource deep entity resolution with transfer and active learning. In *ACL*, pages 5851–5861, 2019. DOI: 10.18653/v1/p19-1586 102, 103

Hideki Kawai, Hector Garcia-Molina, Omar Benjelloun, David Menestrina, Euijong Whang, and Heng Gong. P-Swoosh: Parallel algorithm for generic entity resolution. *Technical Report*, Stanford, 2006. 53

Mayank Kejriwal and Daniel P. Miranker. An unsupervised algorithm for learning blocking schemes. In *ICDM*, pages 340–349, 2013. DOI: 10.1109/icdm.2013.60 23, 63, 93

Mayank Kejriwal and Daniel P. Miranker. A two-step blocking scheme learner for scalable link discovery. In *OM*, pages 49–60, 2014. 63

Mayank Kejriwal and Daniel P. Miranker. A DNF blocking scheme learner for heterogeneous datasets. *CoRR*, 2015a. 63

Mayank Kejriwal and Daniel P. Miranker. An unsupervised instance matcher for schema-free RDF data. *Journal of Web Semantics*, 35:102–123, 2015b. DOI: 10.1016/j.websem.2015.07.002 57, 75

Batya Kenig and Avigdor Gal. MFIBlocks: An effective blocking algorithm for entity resolution. *Information Systems*, 38(6):908–926, 2013. DOI: 10.1016/j.is.2012.11.008 19, 116

Asif R. Khan and Hector Garcia-Molina. Attribute-based crowd entity resolution. In *CIKM*, pages 549–558, 2016. DOI: 10.1145/2983323.2983831 108

Hung-sik Kim and Dongwon Lee. Parallel linkage. In *CIKM*, pages 283–292, 2007. DOI: 10.1145/1321440.1321482 53

Hung-sik Kim and Dongwon Lee. HARRA: Fast iterative hashed record linkage for large-scale data collections. In *EDBT*, pages 525–536, 2010. DOI: 10.1145/1739041.1739104 23, 66

Lars Kolb, Andreas Thor, and Erhard Rahm. Load balancing for MapReduce-based entity resolution. In *ICDE*, pages 618–629, 2012a. DOI: 10.1109/icde.2012.22 52

Lars Kolb, Andreas Thor, and Erhard Rahm. Multi-pass sorted neighborhood blocking with MapReduce. *Computer Science—R&D*, 27(1):45–63, 2012b. DOI: 10.1007/s00450-011-0177-x 50

Lars Kolb, Andreas Thor, and Erhard Rahm. Dedoop: Efficient deduplication with hadoop. *PVLDB*, 5(12):1878–1881, 2012c. DOI: 10.14778/2367502.2367527 50

Pradap Konda, Sanjib Das, Paul Suganthan G. C., AnHai Doan, Adel Ardalan, Jeffrey R. Ballard, Han Li, Fatemah Panahi, Haojun Zhang, Jeffrey F. Naughton, et al. Magellan: Toward building entity matching management systems. *PVLDB*, 9(12):1197–1208, 2016. DOI: 10.14778/2994509.2994535 15, 30, 111, 113

Hanna Köpcke and Erhard Rahm. Frameworks for entity matching: A comparison. *Data and Knowledge Engineering*, 69(2):197–210, 2010. DOI: 10.1016/j.datak.2009.10.003 3

Hanna Köpcke, Andreas Thor, and Erhard Rahm. Evaluation of entity resolution approaches on real-world match problems. *PVLDB*, 3(1):484–493, 2010. DOI: 10.14778/1920841.1920904 3, 30

Nick Koudas, Sunita Sarawagi, and Divesh Srivastava. Record linkage: Similarity measures and algorithms. In *SIGMOD*, pages 802–803, 2006. DOI: 10.1145/1142473.1142599 3

Pigi Kouki, Jay Pujara, Christopher Marcum, Laura M. Koehly, and Lise Getoor. Collective entity resolution in familial networks. In *ICDM*, pages 227–236, 2017. DOI: 10.1109/icdm.2017.32 27, 36, 37

Ioannis K. Koumarelas, Thorsten Papenbrock, and Felix Naumann. MDedup: Duplicate detection with matching dependencies. *PVLDB*, 13(5):712–725, 2020. DOI: 10.14778/3377369.3377379 38, 40, 42

Christos Koutras, George Siachamis, Andra Ionescu, Kyriakos Psarakis, Jerry Brons, Marios Fragkoulis, Christoph Lofi, Angela Bonifati, and Asterios Katsifodimos. Valentine: Evaluating matching techniques for dataset discovery. *CoRR*, 2020. 17

Harold W. Kuhn. The Hungarian method for the assignment problem. *Naval Research Logistics Quarterly*, 2(1–2):83–97, 1955. DOI: 10.1002/nav.3800020109 45

Jerome M. Kurtzberg. On approximation methods for the assignment problem. *Journal of the ACM*, 9(4):419–439, 1962. DOI: 10.1145/321138.321140 45

Shrinu Kushagra, Hemant Saxena, Ihab F. Ilyas, and Shai Ben-David. A semi-supervised framework of clustering selection for de-duplication. In *ICDE*, pages 208–219, 2019. DOI: 10.1109/icde.2019.00027 46

Selasi Kwashie, Jixue Liu, Jiuyong Li, Lin Liu, Markus Stumptner, and Lujing Yang. Certus: An effective entity resolution approach with graph differential dependencies (GDDs). *PVLDB*, 12(6):653–666, 2019. DOI: 10.14778/3311880.3311883 74

Simon Lacoste-Julien, Konstantina Palla, Alex Davies, Gjergji Kasneci, Thore Graepel, and Zoubin Ghahramani. Sigma: Simple greedy matching for aligning large knowledge bases. In *KDD*, pages 572–580, 2013. DOI: 10.1145/2487575.2487592 45, 71

Yoonkyong Lee, Mayssam Sayyadian, AnHai Doan, and Arnon Rosenthal. eTuner: Tuning schema matching software using synthetic scenarios. *VLDB Journal*, 16(1):97–122, 2007. DOI: 10.1007/s00778-006-0024-z 17

Oliver Lehmberg, Christian Bizer, and Alexander Brinkmann. Winte.r—A web data integration framework. In *International Semantic Web Conference (Posters, Demos and Industry Tracks)*, 2017. 113

Guoliang Li. Human-in-the-loop data integration. *PVLDB*, 10(12):2006–2017, 2017. DOI: 10.14778/3137765.3137833 108

Guoliang Li, Dong Deng, Jiannan Wang, and Jianhua Feng. PASS-JOIN: A partition-based method for similarity joins. *PVLDB*, 5(3):253–264, 2011. DOI: 10.14778/2078331.2078340 44, 45

Guoliang Li, Yudian Zheng, Ju Fan, Jiannan Wang, and Reynold Cheng. Crowdsourced data management: Overview and challenges. In *SIGMOD*, pages 1711–1716, 2017. DOI: 10.1145/3035918.3054776 106

Han Li, Pradap Konda, Paul Suganthan G. C., AnHai Doan, Benjamin Snyder, Young-choon Park, Ganesh Krishnan, Rohit Deep, and Vijay Raghavendra. MatchCatcher: A debugger for blocking in entity matching. In *EDBT*, pages 193–204, 2018. DOI: 10.5441/002/edbt.2018.18 24

Juanzi Li, Jie Tang, Yi Li, and Qiong Luo. Rimom: A dynamic multistrategy ontology alignment framework. *TKDE*, 21(8):1218–1232, 2009. DOI: 10.1109/tkde.2008.202 58, 71

Lingli Li, Jianzhong Li, and Hong Gao. Rule-based method for entity resolution. *TKDE*, 27(1):250–263, 2015. DOI: 10.1109/tkde.2014.2320713 27, 38, 39, 40

Yuliang Li, Jinfeng Li, Yoshihiko Suhara, AnHai Doan, and Wang-Chiew Tan. Deep entity matching with pre-trained language models. *PVLDB*, 14(1):50–60, 2020. DOI: 10.14778/3421424.3421431 103, 105, 119

Huizhi Liang, Yanzhe Wang, Peter Christen, and Ross W. Gayler. Noise-tolerant approximate blocking for dynamic real-time entity resolution. In *PAKDD*, pages 449–460, 2014. DOI: 10.1007/978-3-319-06605-9_37 93

Ee-Peng Lim, Jaideep Srivastava, Satya Prabhakar, and James Richardson. Entity identification in database integration. *Information Sciences*, 89(1):1–38, 1996. DOI: 10.1016/0020-0255(95)00185-9 27, 39

Yiming Lin, Hongzhi Wang, Jianzhong Li, and Hong Gao. Efficient entity resolution on heterogeneous records. *TKDE*, 32(5):912–926, 2020. DOI: 10.1109/tkde.2019.2898191 75

Kun Ma, Fusen Dong, and Bo Yang. Large-scale schema-free data deduplication approach with adaptive sliding window using MapReduce. *The Computer Journal*, 58(11):3187–3201, 2015. DOI: 10.1093/comjnl/bxv052 22

Yongtao Ma and Thanh Tran. TYPiMatch: Type-specific unsupervised learning of keys and key values for heterogeneous web data integration. In *WSDM*, pages 325–334, 2013. DOI: 10.1145/2433396.2433439 61

Jayant Madhavan and Alon Y. Halevy. Composing mappings among data sources. In *VLDB*, pages 572–583, 2003. DOI: 10.1016/b978-012722442-8/50057-4 16

Jayant Madhavan, Philip A. Bernstein, and Erhard Rahm. Generic schema matching with cupid. In *VLDB*, pages 49–58, 2001. 15

Jayant Madhavan, Shirley Cohen, Xin Luna Dong, Alon Y. Halevy, Shawn R. Jeffery, David Ko, and Cong Yu. Web-scale data integration: You can afford to pay as you go. In *CIDR*, pages 342–350, 2007. 57, 59, 92

Pankaj Malhotra, Puneet Agarwal, and Gautam Shroff. Graph-parallel entity resolution using LSH and IMM. In *EDBT/ICDT Workshops*, pages 41–49, 2014. 53

Willi Mann, Nikolaus Augsten, and Panagiotis Bouros. An empirical evaluation of set similarity join techniques. *PVLDB*, 9(9):636–647, 2016. DOI: 10.14778/2947618.2947620 43, 45

Neil G. Marchant and Benjamin I. P. Rubinstein. In search of an entity resolution OASIS: Optimal asymptotic sequential importance sampling. *PVLDB*, 10(11):1322–1333, 2017. DOI: 10.14778/3137628.3137642 11

Ruhaila Maskat, Norman W. Paton, and Suzanne M. Embury. Pay-as-you-go configuration of entity resolution. *T. Large-Scale Data- and Knowledge-Centered Systems*, 29:40–65, 2016. DOI: 10.1007/978-3-662-54037-4_2 24

Claire Mathieu, Ocan Sankur, and Warren Schudy. Online correlation clustering. In *STACS*, pages 573–584, 2010. DOI: 10.4230/LIPIcs.STACS.2010.2486 95

Andrew McCallum, Kamal Nigam, and Lyle H. Ungar. Efficient clustering of high-dimensional data sets with application to reference matching. In *KDD*, pages 169–178, 2000. DOI: 10.1145/347090.347123 22, 67

W. P. McNeill, Hakan Kardes, and Andrew Borthwick. Dynamic record blocking: Efficient linking of massive databases in mapreduce. In *QDB*, 2012. 65, 78

David G. McVitie and Leslie B. Wilson. Stable marriage assignment for unequal sets. *BIT Numerical Mathematics*, 10(3):295–309, 1970. DOI: 10.1007/bf01934199 45

Venkata Vamsikrishna Meduri, Lucian Popa, Prithviraj Sen, and Mohamed Sarwat. A comprehensive benchmark framework for active learning methods in entity matching. In *SIGMOD*, pages 1133–1147, 2020. DOI: 10.1145/3318464.3380597 32, 33, 34

Sergey Melnik, Hector Garcia-Molina, and Erhard Rahm. Similarity flooding: A versatile graph matching algorithm and its application to schema matching. In *ICDE*, pages 117–128, 2002. DOI: 10.1109/icde.2002.994702 16

David Menestrina, Steven Whang, and Hector Garcia-Molina. Evaluating entity resolution results. *PVLDB*, 3(1):208–219, 2010. DOI: 10.14778/1920841.1920871 11

Demetrio Gomes Mestre, Carlos Eduardo S. Pires, and Dimas C. Nascimento. Adaptive sorted neighborhood blocking for entity matching with MapReduce. In *SAC*, pages 981–987, 2015. DOI: 10.1145/2695664.2695757 50

Matthew Michelson and Craig A. Knoblock. Learning blocking schemes for record linkage. In *AAAI*, pages 440–445, 2006. 12, 21

Tomas Mikolov, Ilya Sutskever, Kai Chen, Gregory S. Corrado, and Jeffrey Dean. Distributed representations of words and phrases and their compositionality. In *NIPS*, pages 3111–3119, 2013. 99

Steven Minton, Claude Nanjo, Craig A. Knoblock, Martin Michalowski, and Matthew Michelson. A heterogeneous field matching method for record linkage. In *ICDM*, pages 314–321, 2005. DOI: 10.1109/icdm.2005.7 76

Alvaro E. Monge and Charles Elkan. The field matching problem: Algorithms and applications. In *KDD*, pages 267–270, 1996. 25, 27

Alvaro E. Monge and Charles Elkan. An efficient domain-independent algorithm for detecting approximately duplicate database records. In *SIGMOD Workshop on Research Issues on Data Mining and Knowledge Discovery*, 1997. 29, 34

Barzan Mozafari, Purnamrita Sarkar, Michael J. Franklin, Michael I. Jordan, and Samuel Madden. Scaling up crowd-sourcing to very large datasets: A case for active learning. *PVLDB*, 8(2):125–136, 2014. DOI: 10.14778/2735471.2735474 33, 109

Sidharth Mudgal, Han Li, Theodoros Rekatsinas, AnHai Doan, Youngchoon Park, Ganesh Krishnan, Rohit Deep, Esteban Arcaute, and Vijay Raghavendra. Deep learning for entity matching: A design space exploration. In *SIGMOD*, pages 19–34, 2018. DOI: 10.1145/3183713.3196926 98, 99, 101, 116

Dimas Cassimiro Nascimento, Carlos Eduardo Santos Pires, and Demetrio Gomes Mestre. Exploiting block co-occurrence to control block sizes for entity resolution. *Knowledge and Information Systems*, pages 1–42, 2019. DOI: 10.1007/s10115-019-01347-0 68

Felix Naumann and Melanie Herschel. *An Introduction to Duplicate Detection. Synthesis Lectures on Data Management*. Morgan & Claypool Publishers, 2010. DOI: 10.2200/s00262ed1v01y201003dtm003 3

Sahand Negahban, Benjamin I. P. Rubinstein, and Jim Gemmell. Scaling multiple-source entity resolution using statistically efficient transfer learning. In *CIKM*, pages 2224–2228, 2012. DOI: 10.1145/2396761.2398606 31

Markus Nentwig, Anika Groß, and Erhard Rahm. Holistic entity clustering for linked data. In *ICDM Workshops*, pages 194–201, 2016. DOI: 10.1109/icdmw.2016.0035 77

Markus Nentwig, Anika Groß, Maximilian Möller, and Erhard Rahm. Distributed holistic clustering on linked data. In *OTM Conferences II*, pages 371–382, 2017a. DOI: 10.1007/978-3-319-69459-7_25 81

Markus Nentwig, Michael Hartung, Axel-Cyrille Ngonga Ngomo, and Erhard Rahm. A survey of current link discovery frameworks. *Semantic Web*, 8(3):419–436, 2017b. DOI: 10.3233/sw-150210 58, 113

Howard B. Newcombe and James M. Kennedy. Record linkage: Making maximum use of the discriminating power of identifying information. *Communications of the ACM*, 5(11):563–566, 1962. DOI: 10.1145/368996.369026 28

Howard B. Newcombe, James M. Kennedy, S. J. Axford, and A. P. James. Automatic linkage of vital records. *Science*, 130:954–959, 1959. DOI: 10.1126/science.130.3381.954 28

Axel-Cyrille Ngonga Ngomo. HELIOS—Execution optimization for link discovery. In *ISWC*, pages 17–32, 2014. DOI: 10.1007/978-3-319-11964-9_2 76

Axel-Cyrille Ngonga Ngomo and Sören Auer. LIMES—A time-efficient approach for large-scale link discovery on the Web of data. In *IJCAI*, pages 2312–2317, 2011. DOI: 10.5591/978-1-57735-516-8/IJCAI11-385 44, 58, 113

Axel-Cyrille Ngonga Ngomo and Klaus Lyko. EAGLE: Efficient active learning of link specifications using genetic programming. In *ESWC*, pages 149–163, 2012. DOI: 10.1007/978-3-642-30284-8_17 74

Axel-Cyrille Ngonga Ngomo, Klaus Lyko, and Victor Christen. COALA—Correlation-aware active learning of link specifications. In *ESWC*, pages 442–456, 2013. DOI: 10.1007/978-3-642-38288-8_30 74

Hao Nie, Xianpei Han, Ben He, Le Sun, Bo Chen, Wei Zhang, Suhui Wu, and Hao Kong. Deep sequence-to-sequence entity matching for heterogeneous entity resolution. In *CIKM*, pages 629–638, 2019. DOI: 10.1145/3357384.3358018 104

Andriy Nikolov, Victoria Uren, and Enrico Motta. KnoFuss: A comprehensive architecture for knowledge fusion. In *K-CAP*, pages 185–186, 2007. DOI: 10.1145/1298406.1298446 113

Andriy Nikolov, Mathieu d'Aquin, and Enrico Motta. Unsupervised learning of link discovery configuration. In *ESWC*, pages 119–133, 2012. DOI: 10.1007/978-3-642-30284-8_15 75

Jordi Nin, Victor Muntés-Mulero, Norbert Martínez-Bazan, and Josep-Lluís Larriba-Pey. On the use of semantic blocking techniques for data cleansing and integration. In *IDEAS*, pages 190–198, 2007. DOI: 10.1109/ideas.2007.4318104 63

Kenji Nozaki, Teruhisa Hochin, and Hiroki Nomiya. Semantic schema matching for string attribute with word vectors and its evaluation. *International Journal of Networked Distributed Computing*, 7(3):100–106, 2019. DOI: 10.2991/ijndc.k.190710.001 100

Peter Ochieng and Swaib Kyanda. Large-scale ontology matching: State-of-the-art analysis. *ACM Computing Surveys*, 51(4):75:1–75:35, 2018. DOI: 10.1145/3211871 58, 71

Kevin O'Hare, Anna Jurek, and Cassio de Campos. A new technique of selecting an optimal blocking method for better record linkage. *Information Systems*, 77:151–166, 2018. DOI: 10.1016/j.is.2018.06.006 24

Byung-Won On, Nick Koudas, Dongwon Lee, and Divesh Srivastava. Group linkage. In *ICDE*, pages 496–505, 2007. DOI: 10.1109/icde.2007.367895 76

Lorena Otero-Cerdeira, Francisco Javier Rodríguez-Martínez, and Alma Gómez-Rodríguez. Ontology matching: A literature review. *Expert Systems with Applications*, 42(2):949–971, 2015. DOI: 10.1016/j.eswa.2014.08.032 58

Fatemah Panahi, Wentao Wu, AnHai Doan, and Jeffrey F. Naughton. Towards interactive debugging of rule-based entity matching. In *EDBT*, pages 354–365, 2017. DOI: 10.5441/002/edbt.2017.32 27, 38, 39

George Papadakis and Wolfgang Nejdl. Efficient entity resolution methods for heterogeneous information spaces. In *ICDE Ph.D. Workshop*, pages 304–307, 2011. DOI: 10.1109/icdew.2011.5767671 64

George Papadakis, Gianluca Demartini, Peter Fankhauser, and Philipp Kärger. The missing links: Discovering hidden same-as links among a billion of triples. In *IIWAS*, pages 453–460, 2010. DOI: 10.1145/1967486.1967557 61, 78

George Papadakis, George Giannakopoulos, Claudia Niederée, Themis Palpanas, and Wolfgang Nejdl. Detecting and exploiting stability in evolving heterogeneous information spaces. In *JCDL*, pages 95–104, 2011a. DOI: 10.1145/1998076.1998094 120

George Papadakis, Ekaterini Ioannou, Claudia Niederée, and Peter Fankhauser. Efficient entity resolution for large heterogeneous information spaces. In *WSDM*, pages 535–544, 2011b. DOI: 10.1145/1935826.1935903 12, 60, 65

George Papadakis, Ekaterini Ioannou, Claudia Niederée, Themis Palpanas, and Wolfgang Nejdl. Eliminating the redundancy in blocking-based entity resolution methods. In *JCDL*, pages 85–94, 2011c. DOI: 10.1145/1998076.1998093 66

George Papadakis, Ekaterini Ioannou, Claudia Niederée, Themis Palpanas, and Wolfgang Nejdl. Beyond 100 million entities: Large-scale blocking-based resolution for heterogeneous data. In *WSDM*, pages 53–62, 2012. DOI: 10.1145/2124295.2124305 60, 61, 118

George Papadakis, Ekaterini Ioannou, Themis Palpanas, Claudia Niederée, and Wolfgang Nejdl. A blocking framework for entity resolution in highly heterogeneous information spaces. *TKDE*, 25(12):2665–2682, 2013. DOI: 10.1109/tkde.2012.150 11, 25, 59, 60, 61, 65

George Papadakis, Georgia Koutrika, Themis Palpanas, and Wolfgang Nejdl. Meta-blocking: Taking entity resolution to the next level. *TKDE*, 26(8):1946–1960, 2014a. DOI: 10.1109/tkde.2013.54 11, 66, 67

George Papadakis, George Papastefanatos, and Georgia Koutrika. Supervised meta-blocking. *PVLDB*, 7(14):1929–1940, 2014b. DOI: 10.14778/2733085.2733098 31, 69

George Papadakis, George Alexiou, George Papastefanatos, and Georgia Koutrika. Schema-agnostic vs. schema-based configurations for blocking methods on homogeneous data. *PVLDB*, 9(4):312–323, 2015. DOI: 10.14778/2856318.2856326 19, 22, 24, 25, 64, 90, 116

George Papadakis, George Papastefanatos, Themis Palpanas, and Manolis Koubarakis. Scaling entity resolution to large, heterogeneous data with enhanced meta-blocking. In *EDBT*, pages 221–232, 2016a. DOI: 10.5441/002/edbt.2016.22 65, 66, 67

George Papadakis, Jonathan Svirsky, Avigdor Gal, and Themis Palpanas. Comparative analysis of approximate blocking techniques for entity resolution. *PVLDB*, 9(9):684–695, 2016b. DOI: 10.14778/2947618.2947624 64, 69, 70, 116

George Papadakis, Konstantina Bereta, Themis Palpanas, and Manolis Koubarakis. Multi-core meta-blocking for big linked data. In *SEMANTICS*, pages 33–40, 2017. DOI: 10.1145/3132218.3132230 80

George Papadakis, Leonidas Tsekouras, Emmanouil Thanos, George Giannakopoulos, Themis Palpanas, and Manolis Koubarakis. The return of JedAI: End-to-end entity resolution for structured and semi-structured data. *PVLDB*, 11(12):1950–1953, 2018. DOI: 10.14778/3229863.3236232 68

George Papadakis, George Mandilaras, Luca Gagliardelli, Giovanni Simonini, Emmanouil Thanos, George Giannakopoulos, Sonia Bergamaschi, Themis Palpanas, and Manolis Koubarakis. Three-dimensional entity resolution with JedAI. *Information Systems*, 93:101565, 2020a. DOI: 10.1016/j.is.2020.101565 91, 113

George Papadakis, Dimitrios Skoutas, Emmanouil Thanos, and Themis Palpanas. Blocking and filtering techniques for entity resolution: A survey. *ACM Computing Surveys*, 53(2):31:1–31:42, 2020b. DOI: 10.1145/3377455 3, 10, 63, 70, 119

Thorsten Papenbrock, Arvid Heise, and Felix Naumann. Progressive duplicate detection. *TKDE*, 27(5):1316–1329, 2015. DOI: 10.1109/tkde.2014.2359666 83, 91

Hanna Pasula, Bhaskara Marthi, Brian Milch, Stuart J. Russell, and Ilya Shpitser. Identity uncertainty and citation matching. In *NIPS*, pages 1401–1408, 2002. 27, 38

Jeffrey Pennington, Richard Socher, and Christopher D. Manning. Glove: Global vectors for word representation. In *EMNLP*, pages 1532–1543, 2014. DOI: 10.3115/v1/d14-1162 99

Maria Pershina, Mohamed Yakout, and Kaushik Chakrabarti. Holistic entity matching across knowledge graphs. In *IEEE Big Data*, pages 1585–1590, 2015. DOI: 10.1109/big-data.2015.7363924 73

Edward H. Porter, William E. Winkler, et al. Approximate string comparison and its effect on an advanced record linkage system. In *Advanced Record Linkage System. U.S. Bureau of the Census, Research Report*, 1997. 27, 28

Anna Primpeli and Christian Bizer. Profiling entity matching benchmark tasks. In *CIKM*, pages 3101–3108, 2020. DOI: 10.1145/3340531.3412781 116

Anna Primpeli, Christian Bizer, and Margret Keuper. Unsupervised bootstrapping of active learning for entity resolution. In *ESWC*, pages 215–231, 2020. DOI: 10.1007/978-3-030-49461-2_13 32

Sven Puhlmann, Melanie Weis, and Felix Naumann. XML duplicate detection using sorted neighborhoods. In *EDBT*, pages 773–791, 2006. DOI: 10.1007/11687238_46 21

Kun Qian, Lucian Popa, and Prithviraj Sen. Active learning for large-scale entity resolution. In *CIKM*, pages 1379–1388, 2017. DOI: 10.1145/3132847.3132949 32, 103

Kun Qian, Lucian Popa, and Prithviraj Sen. Systemer: A human-in-the-loop system for explainable entity resolution. *PVLDB*, 12(12):1794–1797, 2019. DOI: 10.14778/3352063.3352068 113, 120

Jianbin Qin and Chuan Xiao. Pigeonring: A principle for faster thresholded similarity search. *PVLDB*, 12(1):28–42, 2018. DOI: 10.14778/3275536.3275539 44

Alessandro Raffio, Daniele Braga, Stefano Ceri, Paolo Papotti, and Mauricio A. Hernández. Clip: A visual language for explicit schema mappings. In *ICDE*, pages 30–39, 2008. DOI: 10.1109/icde.2008.4497411 16

Banda Ramadan and Peter Christen. Forest-based dynamic sorted neighborhood indexing for real-time entity resolution. In *CIKM*, pages 1787–1790, 2014. DOI: 10.1145/2661829.2661869 83, 92

Banda Ramadan and Peter Christen. Unsupervised blocking key selection for real-time entity resolution. In *PAKDD*, pages 574–585, 2015. DOI: 10.1007/978-3-319-18032-8_45 93

Banda Ramadan, Peter Christen, Huizhi Liang, Ross W. Gayler, and David Hawking. Dynamic similarity-aware inverted indexing for real-time entity resolution. In *PAKDD Workshops*, pages 47–58, 2013. DOI: 10.1007/978-3-642-40319-4_5 92

Banda Ramadan, Peter Christen, Huizhi Liang, and Ross W. Gayler. Dynamic sorted neighborhood indexing for real-time entity resolution. *Journal of Data and Information Quality*, 6(4):15:1–15:29, 2015. DOI: 10.1145/2816821 92

Vibhor Rastogi, Nilesh N. Dalvi, and Minos N. Garofalakis. Large-scale collective entity matching. *PVLDB*, 4(4):208–218, 2011. DOI: 10.14778/1938545.1938546 36, 53

Pradeep Ravikumar and William W. Cohen. A hierarchical graphical model for record linkage. In *UAI*, pages 454–461, 2004. 27, 28

Russell Reas, Steve Ash, Rob Barton, and Andrew Borthwick. Superpart: Supervised graph partitioning for record linkage. In *ICDM*, pages 387–396, 2018. DOI: 10.1109/icdm.2018.00054 48

Orion Fausto Reyes-Galaviz, Witold Pedrycz, Ziyue He, and Nick J. Pizzi. A supervised gradient-based learning algorithm for optimized entity resolution. *Data and Knowledge Engineering*, 112:106–129, 2017. DOI: 10.1016/j.datak.2017.10.004 15, 27, 29

Marco Túlio Ribeiro, Sameer Singh, and Carlos Guestrin. "Why should I trust you?": Explaining the predictions of any classifier. In *KDD*, pages 1135–1144, 2016. DOI: 10.18653/v1/n16-3020 120

Stephen V. Rice. Braided AVL trees for efficient event sets and ranked sets in the simscript III simulation programming language. In *Western MultiConference on Computer Simulation*, pages 150–155, 2007. 93

Sebastian Riedel, Limin Yao, Andrew McCallum, and Benjamin M. Marlin. Relation extraction with matrix factorization and universal schemas. In *NAACL*, pages 74–84, 2013. 59

Carlos R. Rivero and David Ruiz. Selecting suitable configurations for automated link discovery. In *SAC*, pages 907–914, 2020. DOI: 10.1145/3341105.3373882 74

Chuitian Rong, Wei Lu, Xiaoli Wang, Xiaoyong Du, Yueguo Chen, and Anthony K. H. Tung. Efficient and scalable processing of string similarity join. *TKDE*, 25(10):2217–2230, 2013. DOI: 10.1109/tkde.2012.195 53

Chuitian Rong, Chunbin Lin, Yasin N. Silva, Jianguo Wang, Wei Lu, and Xiaoyong Du. Fast and scalable distributed set similarity joins for big data analytics. In *ICDE*, pages 1059–1070, 2017. DOI: 10.1109/icde.2017.151 53

Alieh Saeedi, Eric Peukert, and Erhard Rahm. Comparative evaluation of distributed clustering schemes for multi-source entity resolution. In *ADBIS*, pages 278–293, 2017. DOI: 10.1007/978-3-319-66917-5_19 48, 54

Alieh Saeedi, Markus Nentwig, Eric Peukert, and Erhard Rahm. Scalable matching and clustering of entities with FAMER. *CSIMQ*, 16:61–83, 2018a. DOI: 10.7250/csimq.2018-16.04 46, 48, 54, 113

Alieh Saeedi, Eric Peukert, and Erhard Rahm. Using link features for entity clustering in knowledge graphs. In *ESWC*, pages 576–592, 2018b. DOI: 10.1007/978-3-319-93417-4_37 48, 54

Alieh Saeedi, Eric Peukert, and Erhard Rahm. Incremental multi-source entity resolution for knowledge graph completion. In *ESWC*, pages 393–408, 2020. DOI: 10.1007/978-3-030-49461-2_23 95

Marcos Antonio Vaz Salles, Jens-Peter Dittrich, Shant Kirakos Karakashian, Olivier René Girard, and Lukas Blunschi. iTrails: Pay-as-you-go information integration in dataspaces. In *VLDB*, pages 663–674, 2007. 92

Sunita Sarawagi and Anuradha Bhamidipaty. Interactive deduplication using active learning. In *KDD*, pages 269–278, 2002. DOI: 10.1145/775047.775087 32, 33

Murat Sariyar, Andreas Borg, and Klaus Pommerening. Controlling false match rates in record linkage using extreme value theory. *Journal of Biomedical Informatics*, 44(4):648–654, 2011. DOI: 10.1016/j.jbi.2011.02.008 113

Anish Das Sarma, Xin Dong, and Alon Y. Halevy. Bootstrapping pay-as-you-go data integration systems. In *SIGMOD*, pages 861–874, 2008. DOI: 10.1145/1376616.1376702 92

Anish Das Sarma, Ankur Jain, Ashwin Machanavajjhala, and Philip Bohannon. An automatic blocking mechanism for large-scale de-duplication tasks. In *CIKM*, pages 1055–1064, 2012. DOI: 10.1145/2396761.2398403 21, 50

Venu Satuluri and Srinivasan Parthasarathy. Bayesian locality sensitive hashing for fast similarity search. *PVLDB*, 5(5):430–441, 2012. DOI: 10.14778/2140436.2140440 44

Tzanina Saveta, Evangelia Daskalaki, Giorgos Flouris, Irini Fundulaki, Melanie Herschel, and Axel-Cyrille Ngonga Ngomo. LANCE: Piercing to the heart of instance matching tools. In *ISWC*, pages 375–391, 2015. DOI: 10.1007/978-3-319-25007-6_22 118

Andrew T. Schneider, Arjun Mukherjee, and Eduard C. Dragut. Leveraging social media signals for record linkage. In *WWW*, pages 1195–1204, 2018. DOI: 10.1145/3178876.3186018 104

Chao Shao, Linmei Hu, Juan-Zi Li, Zhichun Wang, Tong Lee Chung, and Jun-Bo Xia. RiMOM-IM: A novel iterative framework for instance matching. *Journal of Computer Science and Technology*, 31(1):185–197, 2016. DOI: 10.1007/s11390-016-1620-z 71

Jingyu Shao, Qing Wang, and Yu Lin. Skyblocking: Learning blocking schemes on the skyline. *Information Systems*, 85:30–43, 2018. 21

Liangcai Shu, Aiyou Chen, Ming Xiong, and Weiyi Meng. Efficient spectral neighborhood blocking for entity resolution. In *ICDE*, pages 1067–1078, 2011. DOI: 10.1109/icde.2011.5767835 69

Pavel Shvaiko and Jérôme Euzenat. Ontology matching: State-of-the-art and future challenges. *TKDE*, 25(1):158–176, 2013. DOI: 10.1109/tkde.2011.253 58

Giovanni Simonini, Sonia Bergamaschi, and H. V. Jagadish. BLAST: A loosely schema-aware meta-blocking approach for entity resolution. *PVLDB*, 9(12):1173–1184, 2016. DOI: 10.14778/2994509.2994533 59, 67, 69

Giovanni Simonini, George Papadakis, Themis Palpanas, and Sonia Bergamaschi. Schema-agnostic progressive entity resolution. *TKDE*, 31(6):1208–1221, 2019. DOI: 10.1109/tkde.2018.2852763 83, 88, 90, 91

Rohit Singh, Venkata Vamsikrishna Meduri, Ahmed K. Elmagarmid, Samuel Madden, Paolo Papotti, Jorge-Arnulfo Quiané-Ruiz, Armando Solar-Lezama, and Nan Tang. Synthesizing entity matching rules by examples. *PVLDB*, 11(2):189–202, 2017. DOI: 10.14778/3149193.3149199 38, 39, 41

Parag Singla and Pedro M. Domingos. Entity resolution with Markov logic. In *ICDM*, pages 572–582, 2006. DOI: 10.1109/icdm.2006.65 27, 37

Yannis Sismanis, Ling Wang, Ariel Fuxman, Peter J. Haas, and Berthold Reinwald. Resolution-aware query answering for business intelligence. In *ICDE*, pages 976–987, 2009. DOI: 10.1109/icde.2009.81 95

Dezhao Song and Jeff Heflin. Automatically generating data linkages using a domain-independent candidate selection approach. In *ISWC*, pages 649–664, 2011. DOI: 10.1007/978-3-642-25073-6_41 62

Wee Meng Soon, Hwee Tou Ng, and Chung Yong Lim. A machine learning approach to coreference resolution of noun phrases. *Computational Linguistics*, 27(4):521–544, 2001. DOI: 10.1162/089120101753342653 57

Kostas Stefanidis, Vassilis Christophides, and Vasilis Efthymiou. Web-scale blocking, iterative and progressive entity resolution. In *ICDE*, pages 1459–1462, 2017. DOI: 10.1109/icde.2017.214 11, 12

Rebecca C. Steorts, Samuel L. Ventura, Mauricio Sadinle, and Stephen E. Fienberg. A comparison of blocking methods for record linkage. In *Privacy in Statistical Databases*, pages 253–268, 2014. DOI: 10.1007/978-3-319-11257-2_20 23, 69

Giorgos Stoilos, Giorgos B. Stamou, and Stefanos D. Kollias. A string metric for ontology alignment. In *ISWC*, pages 624–637, 2005. DOI: 10.1007/11574620_45 114

Weifeng Su, Jiying Wang, and Frederick H. Lochovsky. Record matching over query results from multiple web databases. *TKDE*, 22(4):578–589, 2010. DOI: 10.1109/tkde.2009.90 94

Fabian M. Suchanek, Serge Abiteboul, and Pierre Senellart. PARIS: Probabilistic alignment of relations, instances, and schema. *PVLDB*, 5(3):157–168, 2011. DOI: 10.14778/2078331.2078332 71, 72

John R. Talburt and Yinle Zhou. A practical guide to entity resolution with OYSTER. In *Handbook of Data Quality, Research and Practice*, pages 235–270. Springer, 2013. DOI: 10.1007/978-3-642-36257-6_11 113

Yufei Tao. Entity matching with active monotone classification. In *ACM PODS*, pages 49–62, 2018. DOI: 10.1145/3196959.3196984 27, 33, 34

Yufei Tao, Ke Yi, Cheng Sheng, and Panos Kalnis. Quality and efficiency in high dimensional nearest neighbor search. In *SIGMOD*, pages 563–576, 2009. DOI: 10.1145/1559845.1559905 44

Sheila Tejada, Craig A. Knoblock, and Steven Minton. Learning object identification rules for information integration. *Information Systems*, 26(8):607–633, 2001. DOI: 10.1016/s0306-4379(01)00042-4 38

Sheila Tejada, Craig A. Knoblock, and Steven Minton. Learning domain-independent string transformation weights for high accuracy object identification. In *KDD*, pages 350–359, 2002. DOI: 10.1145/775047.775099 16, 33

Kai Sheng Teong, Lay-Ki Soon, and Tin Tin Su. Schema-agnostic entity matching using pre-trained language models. In *CIKM*, pages 2241–2244, 2020. DOI: 10.1145/3340531.3412131 103

Burkhard Stiller Thomas Bocek, Ela Hunt. Fast similarity search in large dictionaries. *Technical Report ifi-2007.02*, Department of Informatics, University of Zurich, April 2007. http://fastss.csg.uzh.ch/ 45

Kristina Toutanova, Danqi Chen, Patrick Pantel, Hoifung Poon, Pallavi Choudhury, and Michael Gamon. Representing text for joint embedding of text and knowledge bases. In *EMNLP*, pages 1499–1509, 2015. DOI: 10.18653/v1/d15-1174 60

Stijn Marinus Van Dongen. Graph clustering by flow simulation. Ph.D. thesis, Utrecht University, 2000. 46

Patrick Verga and Andrew McCallum. Row-less universal schema. In *ACL*, pages 63–68, 2016. DOI: 10.18653/v1/w16-1312 60

Rares Vernica, Michael J. Carey, and Chen Li. Efficient parallel set-similarity joins using MapReduce. In *SIGMOD*, pages 495–506, 2010. DOI: 10.1145/1807167.1807222 53

Vasilis Verroios and Hector Garcia-Molina. Entity resolution with crowd errors. In *ICDE*, pages 219–230, 2015. DOI: 10.1109/icde.2015.7113286 106, 108

Vasilis Verroios, Hector Garcia-Molina, and Yannis Papakonstantinou. Waldo: An adaptive human interface for crowd entity resolution. In *SIGMOD*, pages 1133–1148, 2017. DOI: 10.1145/3035918.3035931 107

Vassilios S. Verykios, George V. Moustakides, and Mohamed G. Elfeky. A Bayesian decision model for cost optimal record matching. *VLDB Journal*, 12(1):28–40, 2003. DOI: 10.1007/s00778-002-0072-y 27, 28

Norases Vesdapunt, Kedar Bellare, and Nilesh N. Dalvi. Crowdsourcing algorithms for entity resolution. *PVLDB*, 7(12):1071–1082, 2014. DOI: 10.14778/2732977.2732982 106, 108, 119

Julius Volz, Christian Bizer, Martin Gaedke, and Georgi Kobilarov. Silk—A link discovery framework for the Web of data. In *LDOW*, 2009. 58, 113

Hongzhi Wang, Jianzhong Li, and Hong Gao. Efficient entity resolution based on subgraph cohesion. *Knowledge and Information Systems*, 46(2):285–314, 2016a. DOI: 10.1007/s10115-015-0818-7 48

Jiannan Wang, Guoliang Li, and Jianhua Feng. Trie-join: Efficient trie-based string similarity joins with edit-distance constraints. *PVLDB*, 3(1):1219–1230, 2010. DOI: 10.14778/1920841.1920992 44

Jiannan Wang, Guoliang Li, Jeffrey Xu Yu, and Jianhua Feng. Entity matching: How similar is similar. *PVLDB*, 4(10):622–633, 2011. DOI: 10.14778/2021017.2021020 27, 38, 40

Jiannan Wang, Tim Kraska, Michael J. Franklin, and Jianhua Feng. Crowder: Crowdsourcing entity resolution. *PVLDB*, 5(11):1483–1494, 2012a. DOI: 10.14778/2350229.2350263 106, 107

Jiannan Wang, Guoliang Li, and Jianhua Feng. Can we beat the prefix filtering?: An adaptive framework for similarity join and search. In *SIGMOD*, pages 85–96, 2012b. DOI: 10.1145/2213836.2213847 43, 45

Jiannan Wang, Guoliang Li, Tim Kraska, Michael J. Franklin, and Jianhua Feng. Leveraging transitive relations for crowdsourced joins. In *SIGMOD*, pages 229–240, 2013. DOI: 10.1145/2463676.2465280 106, 108

Jiannan Wang, Sanjay Krishnan, Michael J. Franklin, Ken Goldberg, Tim Kraska, and Tova Milo. A sample-and-clean framework for fast and accurate query processing on dirty data. In *SIGMOD*, pages 469–480, 2014. DOI: 10.1145/2588555.2610505 94

Qing Wang, Mingyuan Cui, and Huizhi Liang. Semantic-aware blocking for entity resolution. *TKDE*, 28(1):166–180, 2016b. DOI: 10.1109/tkde.2015.2468711 23

Richard Y. Wang and Stuart E. Madnick. The inter-database instance identification problem in integrating autonomous systems. In *ICDE*, pages 46–55, 1989. DOI: 10.1109/icde.1989.47199 27, 39

Sibo Wang, Xiaokui Xiao, and Chun-Hee Lee. Crowd-based deduplication: An adaptive approach. In *SIGMOD*, pages 1263–1277, 2015. DOI: 10.1145/2723372.2723739 108

Zhengyang Wang, Bunyamin Sisman, Hao Wei, Xin Luna Dong, and Shuiwang Ji. Cordel: A contrastive deep learning approach for entity linkage. *ICDM*, 2020. 102, 105

Steven Whang and Hector Garcia-Molina. Entity resolution with evolving rules. *PVLDB*, 3(1):1326–1337, 2010. DOI: 10.14778/1920841.1921004 95

Steven Euijong Whang and Hector Garcia-Molina. Incremental entity resolution on rules and data. *VLDB Journal*, 23(1):77–102, 2014. DOI: 10.1007/s00778-013-0315-0 95

Steven Euijong Whang, Omar Benjelloun, and Hector Garcia-Molina. Generic entity resolution with negative rules. *VLDB Journal*, 18(6):1261–1277, 2009a. DOI: 10.1007/s00778-009-0136-3 40, 41

Steven Euijong Whang, David Menestrina, Georgia Koutrika, Martin Theobald, and Hector Garcia-Molina. Entity resolution with iterative blocking. In *SIGMOD*, pages 219–232, 2009b. DOI: 10.1145/1559845.1559870 66

Steven Euijong Whang, Peter Lofgren, and Hector Garcia-Molina. Question selection for crowd entity resolution. *PVLDB*, 6(6):349–360, 2013a. DOI: 10.14778/2536336.2536337 106, 108

Steven Euijong Whang, David Marmaros, and Hector Garcia-Molina. Pay-as-you-go entity resolution. *TKDE*, 25(5):1111–1124, 2013b. DOI: 10.1109/tkde.2012.43 83, 85, 88, 89, 90

Derry Tanti Wijaya and Stéphane Bressan. Ricochet: A family of unconstrained algorithms for graph clustering. In *DASFAA*, pages 153–167, 2009. DOI: 10.1007/978-3-642-00887-0_13 46

William E. Winkler. String comparator metrics and enhanced decision rules in the Fellegi–Sunter model of record linkage. In *Proc. of the Section on Survey Research Methods, American Statistical Association*, pages 354–359, 1990. 27, 28

William E. Winkler. Methods for record linkage and Bayesian networks. *Technical Report, Series RRS2002/05*, U.S. Bureau of the Census, 2002. 27, 28

Renzhi Wu, Sanya Chaba, Saurabh Sawlani, Xu Chu, and Saravanan Thirumuruganathan. Zeroer: Entity resolution using zero labeled examples. In *SIGMOD*, pages 1149–1164, 2020. DOI: 10.1145/3318464.3389743 28, 31

Chuan Xiao, Wei Wang, Xuemin Lin, and Jeffrey Xu Yu. Efficient similarity joins for near duplicate detection. In *WWW*, pages 131–140, 2008. DOI: 10.1145/1367497.1367516 43, 44, 45

Vijaya Krishna Yalavarthi, Xiangyu Ke, and Arijit Khan. Select your questions wisely: For entity resolution with crowd errors. In *CIKM*, pages 317–326, 2017. DOI: 10.1145/3132847.3132876 108, 109

Ling-Ling Yan, Renée J. Miller, Laura M. Haas, and Ronald Fagin. Data-driven understanding and refinement of schema mappings. In *SIGMOD*, pages 485–496, 2001. DOI: 10.1145/375663.375729 16

Su Yan, Dongwon Lee, Min-Yen Kan, and C. Lee Giles. Adaptive sorted neighborhood methods for efficient record linkage. In *JCDL*, pages 185–194, 2007. DOI: 10.1145/1255175.1255213 22

Wei Yan, Yuan Xue, and Bradley Malin. Scalable load balancing for MapReduce-based record linkage. In *IPCCC*, pages 1–10, 2013. DOI: 10.1109/pccc.2013.6742785 52

Yan Yan, Stephen Meyles, Aria Haghighi, and Dan Suciu. Entity matching in the wild: A consistent and versatile framework to unify data in industrial applications. In *SIGMOD*, pages 2287–2301, 2020. DOI: 10.1145/3318464.3386143 27, 29, 46

Diego Zardetto, Monica Scannapieco, and Tiziana Catarci. Effective automated object matching. In *ICDE*, pages 757–768, 2010. DOI: 10.1109/icde.2010.5447904 27, 28

Chen Jason Zhang, Rui Meng, Lei Chen, and Feida Zhu. Crowdlink: An error-tolerant model for linking complex records. In *ExploreDB*, pages 15–20, 2015. DOI: 10.1145/2795218.2795222 107

Chi Zhang, Feifei Li, and Jeffrey Jestes. Efficient parallel KNN joins for large data in MapReduce. In *EDBT*, pages 38–49, 2012. DOI: 10.1145/2247596.2247602 77

Dongxiang Zhang, Long Guo, Xiangnan He, Jie Shao, Sai Wu, and Heng Tao Shen. A graph-theoretic fusion framework for unsupervised entity resolution. In *ICDE*, pages 713–724, 2018. DOI: 10.1109/icde.2018.00070 27, 35

Dongxiang Zhang, Yuyang Nie, Sai Wu, Yanyan Shen, and Kian-Lee Tan. Multi-context attention for entity matching. In *WWW*, pages 2634–2640, 2020a. DOI: 10.1145/3366423.3380017 102

Fulin Zhang, Zhipeng Gao, and Kun Niu. A pruning algorithm for meta-blocking based on cumulative weight. *Journal of Physics*, 887, 2017a. DOI: 10.1088/1742-6596/887/1/012058 67

Meihui Zhang, Marios Hadjieleftheriou, Beng C. Ooi, Cecilia Procopiuc, and Divesh Srivastava. Automatic discovery of attributes in relational databases. In *SIGMOD*, pages 109–120, 2011. DOI: 10.1145/1989323.1989336 16

Wei Zhang, Hao Wei, Bunyamin Sisman, Xin Luna Dong, Christos Faloutsos, and David Page. Autoblock: A hands-off blocking framework for entity matching. In *WSDM*, pages 744–752, 2020b. DOI: 10.1145/3336191.3371813 100

Yong Zhang, Xiuxing Li, Jin Wang, Ying Zhang, Chunxiao Xing, and Xiaojie Yuan. An efficient framework for exact set similarity search using tree structure indexes. In *ICDE*, pages 759–770, 2017b. DOI: 10.1109/icde.2017.127 44

Zhenjie Zhang, Marios Hadjieleftheriou, Beng Chin Ooi, and Divesh Srivastava. Bed-Tree: An all-purpose index structure for string similarity search based on edit distance. In *SIGMOD*, pages 915–926, 2010. DOI: 10.1145/1807167.1807266 44

Chen Zhao and Yeye He. Auto-em: End-to-end fuzzy entity-matching using pre-trained deep models and transfer learning. In *WWW*, pages 2413–2424, 2019. DOI: 10.1145/3308558.3313578 102

Huimin Zhao and Sudha Ram. Entity identification for heterogeneous database integration—a multiple classifier system approach and empirical evaluation. *Information Systems*, 30(2):119–132, 2005. DOI: 10.1016/j.is.2003.11.001 27, 30

Linhong Zhu, Majid Ghasemi-Gol, Pedro A. Szekely, Aram Galstyan, and Craig A. Knoblock. Unsupervised entity resolution on multi-type graphs. In *ISWC*, pages 649–667, 2016. DOI: 10.1007/978-3-319-46523-4_39 75, 76

Authors' Biographies

GEORGE PAPADAKIS

George Papadakis is a research fellow at the National and Kapodistrian University of Athens, Greece. He also worked at the NCSR "Demokritos," National Technical University of Athens (NTUA), L3S Research Center, and "Athena" Research Center. He holds a Ph.D. in Computer Science from the University of Hanover and a Diploma in Electrical Computer Engineering from NTUA. His research interest focuses on web data mining.

EKATERINI IOANNOU

Ekaterini Ioannou is an Assistant Professor at Tilburg University, the Netherlands. Prior, she worked as an Assistant Professor at Eindhoven University of Technology, as a Lecturer at the Open University of Cyprus, an adjunct faculty at EPFL in Switzerland, a research collaborator at the Technical University of Crete, and as an Independent Expert for the European Commission. Her research focuses on information integration with an emphasis on the challenges of managing data with uncertainties, heterogeneity or correlations, and, more recently, on achieving a deeper integration of information extraction tasks within databases, and on efficiently retrieving analytics over graphs/hypergraphs with evolving data.

EMANOUIL THANOS

Emanouil Thanos is a Ph.D. candidate at CODeS research group of KU Leuven, under the supervision of Prof. Greet Vanden Berghe. He holds a Diploma in Electrical and Computer Engineering from the National Technical University of Athens and a joint Master in Computational Logic from TU Dresden, FU Bolzano, and UN Lisbon. He has also worked as a research associate at National ICT Australia and the University of Athens. His research interests focus on combinatorial optimization and operations research.

THEMIS PALPANAS

Themis Palpanas is Senior Member of the French University Institute (IUF), and Professor of Computer Science at the University of Paris (France) where he is director of the Data Intelligence Institute of Paris (diiP), and of the Data Intensive and Knowledge Oriented Systems (diNo) group. He is the author of two French patents and nine U.S. patents, three of which have been implemented in world-leading commercial data management products. He is the recipient of three Best Paper awards and the IBM Shared University Research (SUR) Award. He is currently serving in the Board of Trustees for the Very Large Data Bases (VLDB) Endowment, as Editor in Chief for *BDR Journal*, Editorial Advisory Board member for *IS Journal*, and in the Senior Program Committee of SIGMOD 2021.

Printed in the United States
by Baker & Taylor Publisher Services